EDGAR ALLAN POE'S
Charleston

EDGAR ALLAN POE'S
Charleston

CHRISTOPHER BYRD DOWNEY

THE
History
PRESS

Published by The History Press
Charleston, SC
www.historypress.com

Front cover, bottom: *Panorama of Charleston* by John William Hill. *Courtesy of the Gibbes Museum of Art.*

First published 2020

Manufactured in the United States

ISBN 9781467142021

Library of Congress Control Number: 2019951875

For my dad.

CONTENTS

PREFACE

*E*dgar Allan Poe first entered my life as a welcome break from my middle school's other required reading, like the works of Nathaniel Hawthorne and Thomas Hardy, which the twelve-year-old version of me found quite mundane. Poe's tales of premature burials, spectral birds and torture chambers were unlike anything I had ever read, and his stories ignited my young imagination. When I entered my moody teen years, feeling misunderstood and marginalized, Poe held a whole new relevance for me as the embodiment and literal representation of my teenage awkwardness and angst. And now, as an adult and sometimes writer, I just like to read and research Poe for the simple pleasure it brings me.

You will probably not be too surprised to learn that a Poe fan like myself calls Halloween his favorite holiday. As the author of two books about the history of piracy, my Halloween costume has been a familiar and predictable one for years—a pirate. Part Jack Sparrow and part Stede Bonnet, the gentleman pirate, my costume straddles a broad line between Disney and researched historical accuracy. One year, I did tweak my pirate costume just the slightest by adding a powdered wig, and I celebrated Halloween as a generic, nondescript Colonial America founding father. Most people identified me as George Washington, but I fancied myself more of a Charles Cotesworth Pinckney.

My office hosts an annual costume contest, and when Halloween fell on a Sunday a few years ago, we celebrated two days early on Friday, the 29th. In more than ten years, I had never placed, much less won, the costume contest with either my pirate or my generic, nondescript Colonial America founding father costumes, and I decided to try something new. I had been reading Poe, as tends to be a tradition for me at that time of year, and it inspired me to do a little research about Poe's time in Charleston. This turned out to be the genesis of this book. After spending most of that October Poe-obsessed, I made the bold decision to dress up as Poe for the costume contest. I considered the plan bold because I was concerned that many of my coworkers would not recognize my costume. It turned out that my premonition was well founded.

The costume itself was simple. At a local secondhand clothing store, I found a weather-worn, tight-fitting black coat with long tails and a matching vest. A long piece of silk wrapped several times and tied in a knot around the upturned collar of an un-ironed white linen shirt mimicked the nineteenth-century style found in surviving Poe photographs. I grew out my facial hair for several weeks and then shaved to leave only what was certainly one of the creepiest looking mustaches that any man has ever sported. To imitate the brooding, melancholy visage of Poe, my wife helped apply dull white foundation to my face and dark eyeliner beneath my eyes. Born without even the hint of a curl, and an ever-growing grey tide in my bodiless hair, my coiffure posed some real difficulties. But with the assistance of some novelty coal black–colored hairspray purchased at a Halloween store, I was able to form, or more accurately shellac, my hair to resemble Poe's long part and wave. With as somber of a look as I could muster and carrying a stuffed raven that I bought online, I nervously headed to the office.

The contest was a disaster for me. As I paraded past the judges, I could see the confusion in their eyes. Whether they were just not literary fans or whether my costume was just that poorly conceived, I cannot be sure, but I did later see the notes of one of the judges. Next to my name was written "zombie?" Humiliating. Needless to say, I did not win any prizes, and I retreated to my desk to hide out for the rest of the day.

Late that afternoon, I received a call from a friend whose car had broken down on a rural road on the outskirts of Charleston County. His car needed to be towed and he asked if I could pick him up. More than anxious to leave the office and put the day's disappointments behind me, I readily agreed.

The long drive to pick up my friend turned out to be therapeutic. The air was autumn-like, and I rolled down the windows, opened the sunroof and turned up the Halloween music playing on the radio. "The Monster Mash" and "Werewolves of London" blared, and my spirits started to improve as I sang along and sped through the pine forests and countryside outside of the city.

Making the last turn before reaching my friend, I found that traffic had backed up for nearly a mile from his location. The flashing lights of police cars and tow trucks lit up the roadway, and I quickly realized that an accident had occurred in the stop-and-go, rubbernecking traffic that was trying to skirt around my friend's disabled car. Trying to get as close as possible, I drove slowly and uncomfortably along the grassy shoulder past frustrated drivers who were anxious to get home and start their weekend. I continued until a ravine stopped my progress and then determined to walk the last few hundred feet to my friend's rescue.

As I got out of my car, I immediately sensed the eyes upon me. Confused stares and pointed fingers from those trapped in their cars fell on me as I walked the solid white line of the road. "What is their problem?" I wondered. Did they think I was abandoning my car and somehow cheating my way out of the traffic jam? I increased my pace and tried to ignore the gawkers.

And then I saw it. I caught a glimpse of my reflection in a car's window. I was a monster. The long ride with the windows rolled down had wreaked havoc on my hair. Several large chunks of my black painted hair had broken loose and stood upright in an uneven pattern around my head. Unconscious wipes of my face had smeared my dark eyeliner and pulled it in streaks away from my eyes, bleeding into the paste-white foundation. I looked like a cross between the Joker and Robert Smith of The Cure, circa the *Disintegration* album. And, of course, I was still in full costume—vest, jacket and wrapped silk scarf, which made my appearance even more ridiculous and frightening. It was still two days until Halloween, so most of those observing me probably did not process that I was dressed up in a costume. Their perception was just that of an aberration walking on the side of the road. Maybe some thought I was a ghost.

And then I realized, I had done it. I had pulled off Edgar Allan Poe. My costume may not have matched Poe's physical appearance, but walking down the side of that road, I had channeled Poe, or at least a big piece of the complex person I discovered writing this book—misunderstood, misinterpreted, misconstrued, misrepresented. A contradiction. Both a loner and the center of attention. A guy who just needed to catch a break but too often was his own biggest enemy—unable or unwilling to get out of his own way. A man who in some ways embodied the characters and themes of his stories but in others could not have been furthered removed. With Edgar Allan Poe—like me on that roadside—things are not always what they seem.

For the record, I think Poe would have liked my costume. Still, the next Halloween, I went back to dressing up as a pirate.

Acknowledgements

There are more people to thank for their help with the creation of this book than space allows, but there are a certain few for whom I would like to express my gratitude.

Thank you to Scott Peeples, Delores Schweitzer and the Edgar Allan Poe Library; Jennifer Taylor and Gian Paolo Porcu for their help with the images; Brian Tomlinson, Amanda Holling and the staff of the South Carolina Room at the Charleston Public Library; Karen Stokes and the South Carolina Historical Society; James Hutchisson, Whitney Currin and the Waring Historical Library; the Charleston Library Society, Rick Hatcher, the Unitarian Church of Charleston; Chris Semtner and the Poe Museum of Richmond; Andrea St. Amand, Mark Jones, William Richardson, E. Lee Spence, Lizzie Porcher White, Sailor Byrd and Tina.

1

EDGAR TAKES THE STAGE

From childhood's hour I have not been as others were; I have not seen as others saw; I could not bring my passions from a common spring.
—Edgar Allan Poe, "Alone"

ohn Sollee, manager of Charleston's City Theatre, knew his life was unraveling. His finances were rapidly falling into ruin and, perhaps more distressing, his character was being called into question. The Frenchman's reputation in Charleston society had been hard-earned and now two of his contracted actors—Charles Tubbs and Hayden Edgar—were actively working to discredit and disgrace him.

Tubbs, a musician who had only recently made the transition to the stage, was bitter over the lack of quality roles that Sollee offered him. Relegated to play what were kindly referred to as "useful" roles, Tubbs's acting credits under Sollee's management were much like my own embarrassing childhood credits of non-speaking roles, including my third wise man to the left of the manger performance in my elementary school's Christmas play. But while Tubbs's dissatisfaction was rooted in what he considered a slight by Sollee, or at least a failure by Sollee to recognize his talent, Hayden Edgar's resentment seemed born simply from the generally contrary nature of his own personality—an innately unpleasant disposition that was too often sharpened by intoxication. While a very gifted actor and a staple of the Charleston stage, the off-stage Hayden Edgar had crossed swords and burned bridges with many in Charleston's theater scene.

The year 1797 began full of promise for John Sollee. Having opened the City Theatre three years earlier, Sollee sought to expand his theatrical enterprise outside of Charleston to the newly built Federal Street Theatre in Boston. After a nearly year-long dogged pursuit of talent, and a ballooning payroll, Sollee had been able to secure enough quality actors to form two separate troupes of players with the intention of alternating the two companies during the winter theater seasons between Charleston and Boston. Hoping to protect himself from competition in Boston, Sollee had formed an uneasy alliance that spring with theater managers William Dunlap and John Hodgkinson of New York, whose Old American company also performed seasonally in Boston. The new partners agreed that Sollee would lease Boston's Federal Street Theatre for five years and operate it between the months of November and April, while Dunlap and Hodgkinson would occupy the rival Haymarket Theatre from June to October.

A letter written by Sollee, boasting of his new venture, began appearing in Boston newspapers that summer, expounding, "The two companies already fixed upon are of equal strength, and by exchanging them every winter, it will bring a very satisfactory novelty to the public."

Anxious to gauge the quality of Sollee's new troupe, Dunlap and Hodgkinson required as part of the agreement that Sollee take one of his troupes to perform three nights in New York and the rest of the summer in Philadelphia before taking up residence in Charleston for the winter season. The performances in New York, at the John Street Theatre, were a financial and critical success, but as the group prepared to make the trip to the City of Brotherly Love to finish out the summer season, news of a yellow fever outbreak in Philadelphia reached New York. Too early to head south to Charleston, where the summer heat made it impractical to hold performances until late autumn, Sollee made the ill-fated decision to stay in New York, renew his lease and continue his run at the John Street Theatre. Ill-fated because the Thomas Wignell–managed acting troupe of Philadelphia, fleeing the yellow fever outbreak, had also just arrived in New York and secured a three-month lease at the Greenwich Street Theatre, just a few blocks from the John Street Theatre.

Sollee's troupe did count among its members two of the most famous leading ladies in America: Elizabeth Kemble Whitlock and Louisa Fontenelle Williamson. Whitlock, a dynamic and versatile actress, was already a legend of the American stage by 1797 and, accompanied by her husband, Charles, who oddly split time between acting and practicing dentistry, had been aggressively recruited by Sollee in Boston. Mrs. Whitlock's counterpart and sometimes rival Elizabeth Williamson was new to the American stage, but she had been described by poet Robert Treat Paine the previous year at her American debut in Boston as "the most astonishing and brilliant display of theatrical genius ever exhibited in America." In the first few weeks in New York, Williamson's and Whitlock's popularity alone filled the seats at the John Street Theatre.

But Sollee lacked a leading man to compete with those of Wignell's company, which included James Fernell and Thomas Cooper, who were both wildly popular with the public. As summer faded into fall, this lack of a strong leading man began to thin the crowds at the John Street Theatre. To make matters worse, Sollee's boon of two strong leading ladies quickly turned to burden when he found himself defending his casting choices of both Whitlock and Williamson to the New York press, as fans of both actresses wrote scathing letters to newspapers, complaining that their favorite was not receiving enough leading roles and stage time.

By late September, more and more empty seats were appearing at the John Street Theatre. Even Sollee's New York premiere of the patriotic piece *The Battle of Bunker Hill and the Death of General Warren,* which was attended by President John Adams, could not rescue the sinking box office returns. William Dunlap, who later in life described Sollee in his book *History of the American Theatre* as "a very genteel, acute Frenchman," was much less flattering in the autumn of 1797 when writing to John Hodgkinson. Of their new partner's troubles, he stated, "Sollee is almost aground" and "is in debt to every body." In early October, Sollee decided to cut his losses and announced his premature closing at the John Street Theatre. Stretching his finances even thinner, Sollee begrudgingly advanced his demoralized players money to make the long journey to Charleston.

Much like Boston, Charleston's theatrical landscape in the waning years of the eighteenth century was dominated by two rival theaters: the Charleston Theatre and Sollee's City Theatre, also referred to as the French Theatre. Sollee, of Huguenot descent, had arrived in Charleston in late 1791, escaping the Reign of Terror of the French Revolution. With refugees fleeing both the French Revolution and the ongoing slave revolt in Haiti, the French population in late-eighteenth-century Charleston was swelling, and though Sollee was described by William Dunlap as "imperfectly acquainted with the English language, and utterly unacquainted with English literature, especially dramatic," Sollee was savvy enough to recognize a good business opportunity when one presented itself. With the long tradition of theater among the French, a guileful Sollee reasoned that a French theater in

Charleston could thrive, even while running in competition with the nearby Charleston Theatre, which catered to "English tastes."

Constructed in 1794 on the ruins of a theater built by David Douglass in 1773 and destroyed by fire in 1782, Sollee's City Theatre was located on Church Street, south of its intersection with Broad Street. Today, you can find tourists prowling Church Street, seeking out the fictitious tenement Catfish Row, made famous by George Gershwin's opera *Porgy and Bess*, near the site where Sollee's theater once stood. Records show that Sollee paid £700 for the lot, which paralleled the west side of Church Street for 50 feet and 6 inches and ran from east to west for 245 feet. The theater was built on the western portion of the lot with a passageway running from Church Street to the theater's doors. Sollee, apparently aware of his shortcomings and inexperience in managing a theater, wisely hired another Frenchman and fellow refugee, the multitalented actor Alexandre Placide, to manage the operations of the City Theatre.

Alexandre Placide.

Placide, who had fled the slave revolt in Haiti, arrived in Charleston in 1791. Billing himself as *Danseur and Sauter du Roi* after performing for both King Louis XV and Louis XVI in Paris, Placide counted tightrope walking and acrobatics among his stage talents. In addition to his performing and theater management, the industrious Placide also managed Vauxhall, a pleasure garden and event venue located at the northeast corner of Broad and Legare Streets at the site of present-day Cathedral of St. John the Baptist. Vauxhall offered Charlestonians a variety of entertainment, including concerts, masked balls, public baths and even ice cream within its gardens "after the Parisian manner."

On November 7, 1797, Placide took centerstage at the City Theatre and announced the official start to the winter season to a sold-out crowd. Ticket sales remained steady for the first few weeks of the season, and by late November, when attendance had not shown any sign of slowing, Sollee decided that his City Theatre was not proving to be a sufficient space. Essentially one large, open room with a low-raised stage, the

City Theatre did not offer adequate capacity and was not particularly comfortable for theatergoers.

In December, when Sollee learned that the lease at the rival Charleston Theatre had become available with the departure of Thomas West's company at the end of its season, the already financially strapped Sollee moved quickly to secure the vacant theater's lease. Located at Broad and New Streets, adjacent to Savage's Green, the Charleston Theatre, with its seating capacity of twelve hundred and three tiers of boxes, was exquisite in design compared to the City Theatre. And while Sollee's announcement of upcoming performances in the Charleston Theatre in the *State Gazette* declared, "The largeness and elegance of that house will give the ample scope for the merits of the performers," Sollee's decision to carry the note on two theater leases may have been partially motivated by self-preservation. Sollee reasoned that by holding the lease on both of Charleston's rival theaters, he could be sure to remove any threat of competition.

By early January, the company had moved into the spacious Charleston Theatre just in time to perform a new allegorical piece titled *Americania and Eleutheria* written by an unnamed Charlestonian playwright. Pruned from five acts to two for time constraints, the play celebrated American liberty with dancing nymphs, satyrs and even an appearance by Lucifer. Though reviews were mixed, the piece proved very popular with the Charleston public, since it had been written by a local and the performances were consistently sold out. Unfortunately, only two weeks after moving into the Charleston Theatre, a fire broke out backstage during a performance, causing enough damage that the troupe was forced to shuffle back to the City Theatre.

When performances of *Americania and Eleutheria* resumed at the City Theatre, hints of the cumulative strain on Sollee's finances first became apparent, with one critic keenly noting the cheapness of the play's scenery in a review in the *Charleston Gazette*: "Some of the scenery did not appear to be well calculated to give all the effect that the more grand and interesting passages were susceptible of." Unfortunately, those shoddy stage props were only a shadow of Sollee's impending financial implosion. Saddled with debt from the failures in New York the previous summer, the cost of leasing two theaters and repairing after the fire at the Charleston Theatre, Sollee was finding it more and more difficult to keep his head above water. By late February, with his debt mounting, Sollee fell a week behind in paying his actors, and the situation got even worse for John Sollee. Much worse. Nervous and wary of his fiscal soundness, a mutiny began to take form among Sollee's company, and the popular acting couple, the Whitlocks, provided the first public voices of dissent.

After the previous summer's disappointments in New York, the Whitlocks planned to abandon the troupe and return to Boston, but Sollee managed to convince the couple to come to Charleston. In exchange, a deal was struck with Charles Whitlock, wherein Charles was promised that he would only play parts that he had previously performed, meaning he would not have to learn and rehearse new roles. This would permit Charles time to pursue his other passion—dentistry. However, Sollee had gone back on his word and assigned Charles to play lead characters in complicated Shakespearean pieces that Charles had not previously performed. Sollee's broken promise, coupled with the delay in paying the company, pushed the agitated Whitlocks to retaliate, threatening not to perform without immediate payment. Other members of the troupe, including Hayden Edgar and Charles Tubbs, followed suit and threatened outright revolt unless immediately paid. The dispute grew increasingly ugly and began to play out in Charleston's streets and newspapers.

Sollee's company fractured into two factions: those like the Whitlocks, Edgar and Tubbs, demanding their salaries, and those who remained loyal to their manager, including Alexandre Placide. Sollee offered to work out a payment plan, but Edgar, Tubbs and the Whitlocks would accept nothing less than what they considered full and complete payment.

Letters attacking Sollee's character, signed with pseudonyms, began appearing in Charleston newspapers. These pseudonyms grew increasingly longer and more creative as the days passed, eventually prompting one paper to announce, "To Correspondents: No communication respecting the late misunderstanding in the theatre corps can appear in this *Gazette* unless the name of the author is left with the publishers."

A letter signed with the protracted pseudonym Franciscus Decimus Coriolanus William decried Sollee as a "thief" and listed the specific amount of back pay owed to each actor. This elicited an angry response from Sollee, who called out Tubbs as the author and wrote, "The piece inserted in the *State Gazette* of yesterday and signed by Franciscus Decimus Coriolanus William, ending in Tubbs…would have been beneath my notice, by its meanness, but I am inculpated with owing him forty-three dollars for salary." Sollee explained that his rebellious actors, particularly Tubbs, were not due payment at all, but rather were in debt to Sollee for the money he had advanced for travel expenses from New York to Charleston the previous October. Sollee referred to Tubbs as "vermin" and listed his total debt for expenses, including those of his wife and stepdaughter, who were also part of the company, as ninety-eight dollars. Further, Sollee accused Tubbs of stealing wardrobe, specifically a dress made for his stepdaughter for her role in *Harlequin Skeleton*, an offense for which Sollee said he could have Tubbs "arrested and put in prison." He reminded Tubbs that he was a stranger in Charleston and "without friends" who could bail him out of jail.

As for Hayden Edgar, Sollee wrote succinctly that Edgar was owed nothing because, according to Sollee, Edgar had been "discharged from the Company a week before…having been intoxicated and unable to perform for three nights running." In regard to the possibility of a reconciliation with Edgar, Sollee declared, "I would rather see an annihilation of my theatre than receive such a dangerous man."

That same day, another letter, most likely also written by Sollee but signed by those of the troupe loyal to Sollee, including Placide, appeared in the *City Gazette and Daily Advertiser*, "We the undersigned, acknowledge that Mr. Sollee has proposed to those of the performers who would insist upon having their money for last week's salaries, to pay them…provided that the performers would give also a security for the payment of their benefit nights charges."

Theater tradition held that each leading actor was given at least one night's performance each season as his or her "benefit." The beneficiary chose the pieces to be performed on a benefit night and received all profits for the evening, minus the house's expenses. Benefit performances were generally well attended, particularly for popular actors, as the public knew that a benefit was a large portion of an actor's income, and attendance was a way to give support and show admiration. Consequently, Charleston was shocked to read the announcement in the newspaper the following day: "Mrs. Whitlock respectfully informs the public and her friends that her Benefit is postponed during the Manager's pleasure." The Whitlocks were playing hardball.

A pertinacious Sollee was determined to hold the already rehearsed benefit performances and continued to negotiate with the Whitlocks throughout the following day. Meanwhile, Tubbs and Edgar took to the streets of Charleston, passing out handbills that stated the theater would be closed, "since the best players don't perform any more." When Edgar encountered Placide exiting an apothecary shop, he encouraged Placide to join the mutiny against Sollee, but the Frenchman told Edgar, "It was not delicate in a first-rate actor of Charleston to fulfill the functions of a black-guard, in giving out in the streets such hand-bills." Placide grabbed the handbill from Edgar and spit on it. Edgar raised his cane, and one of his companions placed a threatening fist under Placide's nose. Placide coolly explained to Edgar that "it was ungenerous for two to attack one." Hostilities ceased when Placide returned inside the apothecary and then reemerged with a borrowed cane, causing Edgar and his companion to beat a hasty retreat to the opposite side of the street.

Only hours before the curtain was to be raised, Sollee was finally able to reach a financial agreement with Elizabeth and Charles Whitlock, and both were rushed to the theater and hurriedly dressed in costume. Edgar and Tubbs's handbills had their desired effect, and only a small crowd was in attendance when Elizabeth Whitlock's benefit performance began. Early in the first act, a loud hissing could be heard coming from the nearly empty gallery. Placide and several of the stagehands rushed upstairs and discovered an intoxicated Edgar hiding behind the balustrade, hissing mockingly toward the stage. Recognizing that he was outnumbered, Edgar scampered quickly out of the theater and into the street.

The performance continued despite the interruption, but the damage had been done. The dismal box office returns of the benefit night and the poorly attended following few nights were the last straw. Sollee's finances were in ruin. The negative publicity generated by Edgar and Tubbs meant Sollee was finding it more and more difficult to borrow money from spooked creditors. Adding insult to injury, news reached Charleston that on February 3, the Federal Theatre in Boston had burned to the ground. Sollee's theater exchange program, for which he had harbored so much hope and spent so much money, came to a crushing end.

A few weeks later, the following announcement appeared in the *City Gazette*: "Sheriff's Sales....A Lot of Land, situate on the West side of Church-Street, on which the City Theatre now stands....To be sold under Execution as the property of John Sollee....Conditions, Cash."

The announcement was printed prematurely. Sollee had already arranged to sell the City Theatre and the Charleston Theatre leases to Placide the day before. Sollee indulged in self-pity in one last letter to the *City Gazette* on March 5: "I may venture to make the public the following declaration...no man has met with more misfortunes, than I since four years. However, I have persevered with indefatigable labor, even to astonish every one who knows me. During three months to come, it will be increased still, so as to enable me to make the following bargain with my creditors to who I owe pretty nearly 11,000 dollars."

The 1797–98 Charleston winter theater season makes a compelling story and is probably worthy of its own book, though I have only shared a small taste. The dozens of letters printed in the newspaper could be scripted into a melodrama to rival any stage production that Sollee's troupe might have performed that season. If you have the time and the means, I encourage you to read through the Charleston newspapers of that winter and enjoy the show. But you are probably thinking, "I am deep into the first chapter of a book about Edgar Allan Poe, and the author hasn't even mentioned Poe yet." So, please, allow me to close the circle.

Just like I perused those old Charleston newspapers for articles and letters regarding that volatile winter theater season, it seems that Edgar Allan Poe did the same in Charleston in 1828. We will examine the evidence of Poe's research of these Charleston newspapers in a later chapter, but first, let me share with you the reason for Poe's interest in this melodrama.

Charles Tubbs's stepdaughter, the owner of that *Harlequin* dress, was a ten-year-old named Eliza Arnold. Though very young, Eliza was already a veteran of the stage when she made her Charleston debut in 1797, singing "The Market Lass" at the City Theatre. While she would appear in nearly three hundred parts in her brief career, and while her talents would be critically acclaimed and universally celebrated, it is for her role as mother of Edgar Allan Poe that she is most remembered.

On January 3, 1796, Eliza arrived in the United States at the port of Boston onboard the *Outram* and accompanied by her recently widowed mother, Elizabeth Arnold. Eliza's mother was a product of the repertory system of England and had been scouted in London by Charles Powell, manager of the newly built Federal Street Theatre in Boston. He offered Elizabeth a contract to move to the United States. Joining Eliza and her mother onboard the *Outram* was the disagreeably tempered Charles Tubbs. Little is known of Tubbs, except that he was a musician who played the pianoforte and an aspiring actor, and he was in love with Elizabeth Arnold. The *Massachusetts Mercury* on January 5, 1796, announced their arrival:

> *On Sunday arrived in this Port in the Ship Outram, Capt. Davis, from London, Mrs. Arnold and Daughter from the Theatre Royal, Covent Garden, and Miss Green. Both engaged by Mr. Powell, for the Boston Theatre, Each of the Ladies are tall and genteel—have an expressive Countenance—And Move with a Symetry [sic] unequalled. Mrs. Arnold is about in her four and twentieth year....They will be valuable acquisitions to our Theatre, and we anxiously hope they will be engaged.*

Edgar Allan Poe's mother, Eliza Poe.

Tubbs made a less impressive appearance at the bottom of the same announcement: "Other passengers by Captain Davis, Mr. Tubbs."

American theater was experiencing unprecedented growth in the late eighteenth century, but the institution was still viewed by many as immoral, particularly in New England. A 1750 Puritan-influenced law in Boston made it a crime to perform in, or even attend, a theater. Prior to the Revolutionary War, there were no designated theaters in Boston; however, clever theater enthusiasts in Boston had built the New Exhibition Room, which served as a theater in all but name. Visiting acting companies would skirt the laws in Boston by billing plays as "moral lectures," until the law was finally repealed in 1793.

While the virtuous Puritans of New England were certainly more aggressive toward the theater than the people in other regions of the new United States, there were many people with similar sentiments even as far south as Charleston. In 1794, when a storm destroyed Sollee's still under construction City Theatre, an article printed in the February 24 issue of the *City Gazette* pointed to possible divine retribution being responsible because of the theater's proximity to several houses of worship on Church Street:

> *Wherever God erects a House of Pray'r, The Devil's sure to build a Chapel near!…The proximity of the New French Theatre to the New Church must strike every antiquated gentlewoman as a circumstance highly shocking and indecent. To this alone may be attributed the downfall of that profane temple, intended for nothing but new scenes of riot and debauchery, and for the promotion and encouragement of the Devil and all his Works.*

Any hostility toward the theater among conservatives in Boston in 1796 was at least temporarily forgotten when Elizabeth took the stage for the first time at the Federal Street Theatre. The day after Elizabeth's Boston debut, in which she played Rosetta in the comic opera *Love in a Village*, the *Massachusetts Mercury* reported on her performance, stating, "The theatre never shook with such bursts of applause. Not a heart was sensible of her merits; not a tongue but vibrated in her praise; not a hand but moved in approbation." Three months later, when Elizabeth had her first benefit night in Boston, performing in the lead roles of the romantic melodrama *Mysteries of the Castle* and the musical *Rosina*, her young daughter's meteoric career began in earnest when, in between her performances, Elizabeth led the then nine-year-old Eliza onto the stage, and she sang "The Market Lass." Eliza's performance was an absolute sensation, and the audience was stunned by the little girl's maturity and vocal talents. A star was born. Eliza and her mother made quite an impression on Boston, and Boston, America's largest city at the time, clearly made a strong impression on the pair. Although Eliza would live the typical transient lifestyle of an actress, she would consider Boston her home for the rest of her life.

Eliza and her mother capitalized on their success in Boston, barnstorming theaters throughout New England for nearly a year. During this time, Eliza's mother married Charles Tubbs, and she began billing herself as Elizabeth Tubbs. Eliza continued to grow her repertoire, adding a new song, "Henry's Cottage Maid" and appearing in her first acting roles as Phoebe in *Rosina* and Biddy Belair in *Miss in Her Teens*. In Portland, Maine, Eliza took the stage in what would become her signature role for years to come, Little Pickle in *The Spoiled Child*. A review of Eliza's mother in the *Eastern Herald and Gazette of Maine* mentions Eliza's performance as Little Pickle and flatters her with praise: "But the powers of her daughter, Miss Arnold, astonish us. Add to these her youth, her beauty, her innocence, and a character is composed which has not, and perhaps will not again ever be found on any Theatre. —Lovely child!"

Throughout the spring, while barnstorming theaters in New England, and into the summer, at the John Street Theatre in New York after joining Sollee's company, Eliza's list of roles swelled, built on a wave of adulation and critical praise. But upon arriving in Charleston, perhaps as a harbinger of the troubles to come, Eliza was met with disappointment, learning that Sollee had cast Alexandre Placide's wife, Charlotte, in Eliza's signature role of Little Pickle in *The Spoiled Child* on opening night at the City Theatre. Casting came slowly for Eliza in Charleston, and she played many small "useful" roles, like a walk-on in *The Battle of Bunker Hill and the Death of General Warren* and a dancing nymph in *Americania and Eleutheria* (Charles Tubbs played a dancing nymph as well). But Sollee eventually recognized Eliza's talents and gave her larger parts, including her first Shakespearean role as the Duke of York in *Richard III* and what would turn out to be that infamous role in *Harlequin Skeleton*.

But, of course, just as Eliza's stage time and talents were beginning to blossom in Charleston, Sollee's company fractured, and, through no fault of her own, Eliza found herself an out-of-work member of a mutinous acting troupe. The unpleasant nature of the dissolution of the company and Sollee's threats to arrest her stepfather over her *Harlequin* dress must have been terrifying for ten-year-old Eliza. The experiences of Eliza's short ten years probably made her seem older than her age, but she was still just a child. Many professional actors of the age, even those with a measure of success, lived a near hand-to-mouth existence, so the fact that Eliza's family, entirely composed of actors, was unemployed and hundreds of miles away from home had to be heavy burden for a little girl.

Short on options, the small faction of dissenters from Sollee's company turned to the irascible Hayden Edgar for leadership, and Edgar arranged for the group to sail to Wilmington, North Carolina for a nine-night engagement in late March. In Wilmington, with the greatly reduced company size, Eliza was given much more stage time. Eliza flourished in this new environment, and Hayden Edgar, who declared himself manager of the new company, quickly recognized her talent. The troupe returned to Charleston in early April and reenlisted the Whitlocks and several other local actors, naming their new company the Charleston Comedians. Booking the group at the Charleston Theatre, which had recently been vacated at the end of their former troupe's winter season, the Charleston Comedians opened on April 9 for a three-week run.

Edgar placed Eliza center stage on opening night, casting her in two shows—first, in the familiar role of Biddy Belair in *Miss in Her Teens* and then in a new role as Nancy in *Three Weeks after Marriage*. Two nights later, she played her signature role of Little Pickle in *The Spoiled Child*. Eliza also took on the demanding and adult role of the coy Pink in the comedy *The Young Quaker* to critical acclaim. During their final week in Charleston, Edgar gave Eliza her first benefit night, where she played the leading role of Sophia in

An artist's rendering of the Charleston Theatre, where both of Edgar Allan Poe's parents performed. Opened in 1793 and located at the intersection of present-day Broad and New Streets, the theater boasted a fifty-six-foot circular front stage, three tiers of boxes and a total seating capacity of twelve hundred. *Courtesy of the Waring Historical Library, MUSC, Charleston, SC.*

The Road to Ruin. When the Charleston Comedians closed their Charleston run on May 1, Eliza's life had irrevocably changed. In less than one month, thanks in large part to Hayden Edgar, Eliza had transformed from an ingenue to a professional actress with leading role credits and an impressive catalog of parts.

Still billing themselves as the Charleston Comedians, despite Hayden Edgar staying behind in Charleston, Charles, Elizabeth, Eliza and a few others of the company headed north with the intention of joining Thomas Wade West's Virginia company, which played a summer circuit that included Norfolk, Petersburg, Fredericksburg, Alexandria and Richmond. But while playing small towns in North Carolina to finance their journey to Virginia, tragedy struck when Eliza's mother suddenly became ill while performing in Halifax. Though she initially showed signs of recovering, Elizabeth Tubbs died of yellow fever in late July 1798.

Heartbroken, Eliza spent the next six months with the Virginia company before joining Thomas Wignell's company in Philadelphia in 1799. By 1802, Eliza had rejoined West's Virginia company, and in July 1804, West's company took up residence at the Quarrier's Theatre in Richmond for a short summer season, beginning rehearsals for a new comedy named *Speed the Plow*. Eliza was given the lead opposite a new member of the company who had just arrived in Richmond, a handsome nineteen-year-old named David Poe.

Born in 1784, David was part of a proud and patriotic family from Baltimore. His father, and namesake, was a Revolutionary War hero affectionately known as General Poe, who had funded the cause of liberty from his own pocket, giving $500 to the Marquis de Lafayette when he passed through the city with ragged colonial troops in 1781. When Lafayette returned to Baltimore as part of his celebrated American tour in 1824, he sought General Poe's widow and paid her a handsome tribute to honor her late husband's charity.

Unlike Eliza, David Poe did not have acting in his blood. David had been apprenticed to the law by his father, but he caught the acting bug in his late teens and, disappointingly to his family, decided to abandon his studies, leave Baltimore and pursue a career on the stage. Making his way south, his first professional engagement would come under Alexandre Placide's management in Charleston. He made his debut at the Charleston Theatre on December 1, 1803, in the nonspeaking role of an army officer in the pantomime *La Peyrouse*. On December 5, announced as "his second appearance on any stage," David played his first speaking role of Laertes in *Gustavus Vasa*, and two nights later, he was advanced to the part of Harry Thunder in *Wild Oats*.

Charleston critics were not kind to David Poe. Bouts of stage fright that would haunt him throughout his short career caused him to forget lines and freeze on stage. Awash in nervous energy, he would frequently deliver his lines too quickly and often struggled to enunciate words properly. One critic wrote to the *Charleston Courier* on December 10 after David's debut, stating, "We hope he will excuse our suggesting to him, that speaking slower will not only help him to get rid of those fears more quickly, by making him less subject to lapses, but will improve his delivery, and give meaning and effect to his words. He ought to practice before some judicious friends, and beg of them candidly to set him right, when he is wrong."

David's first professional season under Alexandre Placide's management was clearly difficult with a seemingly steep learning curve. But while punctuated with disappointments and criticism, a few positive reviews of David's performances can be found in Charleston's newspapers of 1804. These seem to show that David performed best in Shakespearean pieces. A February 13 review of his performance in *Richard III* by a Charleston critic writing under the pseudonym Thespis compliments David, saying, "Young Poe in the character of Tressel did more to justify our hopes of him than he has done in any character." A couple of weeks later, Thespis wrote again of another of David's Shakespearean roles: "Young Poe being less than usual under the dominion of that timid modesty which so depresses his powers, acted Don Pedro so respectably as to animate the hopes we have entertained of his future progress."

In the *Charleston Courier* on March 10, a review appears that seems to best define David's debut season in Charleston and summarize audiences' sentiments for the young actor. While the critic chides David for his lackluster performances throughout most of the season, the author does temper the review with some encouragement for David's future: "Young Poe begins to emerge from the abyss of embarrassment in which natural diffidence from his first appearance till but two or three of his last performances had plunged him so deep as to deprive him of all power of exertion. But he must have not only courage but patience—slow rises the actor."

When David arrived in Richmond in the summer of 1804, following his debut season in Charleston, it is possible that he was already familiar with his new costar, perhaps having seen Eliza in one of her off-season performances in Baltimore while still part of Thomas Wignell's company. David perhaps even brought a teenager's celebrity crush on Eliza. The pair spent a great deal of time together in rehearsals that summer in Richmond, working on and developing their onstage chemistry and timing. David performed in several roles in Richmond that were new to him, and, considering his struggles in his debut season in Charleston, he most likely took advantage of all the rehearsal time with Eliza that he could find. The pair would play one another's love interests in several productions that first season, and by the time the 1805–06 winter season began at the newly completed Richmond Theatre, their onstage chemistry had translated into their personal lives. The couple married in Richmond on March 14, 1806.

When the curtain fell for the last time on that 1806 season, the newlyweds decided that it was time for a change, leaving Richmond and heading north. After a short run of performances in theaters in Philadelphia and an outdoor summer theater in New York, Mr. and Mrs. Poe settled in Boston where they performed for the next three seasons. Eliza must have been happy to be back in her adopted hometown and even happier for the opportunity not afforded to many actors of enjoying the stability of living in one place for a relatively long period time. Boston audiences welcomed Eliza and showered her with praise. One review described her as "the favorite of the public, and the delight of the eye."

Unfortunately, David did not fare as well—his stage fright returning and critics once again bashing his performances in the press. A review in the *Centinel* in January 1807, points to David's articulation issues: "He wants however a deliberation and a temperance of speech without which his articulation must ever be too rapid to be discriminate." A review of David's leading role in *The London Merchant* at the Federal Street Theatre in the *Polyanthos* reads, "Of Mr. Poe's Barnwell we expected little satisfaction, and of course were not disappointed." David increasingly turned to alcohol to numb the pain of the criticisms.

On January 30, 1807, Eliza gave birth to a son who David named William Henry Leonard Poe—Henry for short. Two years later, a second child was born, and Eliza was given the choice of the name. Searching her past for influences, Eliza named the baby born on January 19, 1809, Edgar, to honor the ill-tempered, irascible, subversive and all too often intoxicated Hayden Edgar of Charleston. The Hayden Edgar who had sabotaged Sollee's career. The Hayden Edgar who had hissed mockingly from the balustrade at Elizabeth Whitlock's benefit night. The Hayden Edgar who had physically challenged Alexandre Placide in the street. Of course, for Eliza, he was the Hayden Edgar who had changed the trajectory of her stage career when she was only ten years old. The Hayden Edgar who had been the first to truly

An 1807 Boston playbill for a benefit night for Edgar Allan Poe's parents, David and Eliza Poe.

recognize her talents, pushing her center stage after that volatile 1797–98 winter season in Charleston and giving her a first benefit while a member of a rogue troupe called the Charleston Comedians.

The newly arrived Edgar Poe appears to have been an unexpected, or at least unplanned, addition to the Poe family, as David and Eliza were wholly financially unprepared for a second child. Eliza was forced to return to the stage only three weeks after Edgar was born, and David left the company entirely, traveling south to visit family and ask for financial assistance. Declaring that he wanted to abandon acting, "provided I could do any thing else that would give bread to mine," he humbly begged a cousin for a loan of "30, 20, 15, or even $10."

Returning to Boston empty-handed, David moved the family to New York, where David and Eliza both signed on for an engagement at the Park Street Theatre, the largest theater in the United States at the time, with seating for two thousand. Eliza was embraced by New York theatergoers, but David's performances were again panned, and his reviews reached new lows. David was caricatured in the New York press as having a "muffin face," a symptom of his heavy drinking, and he was nicknamed Dan Dilly after mispronouncing the name Dandoli while on stage. David's temperament, poisoned by his alcoholism, raged unfiltered, and he lashed out, even physically threatening several critics who hammered his performances in the New York press.

On October 20, a cast change was announced at the Park Street Theatre due to David's "sudden indisposition," a euphemism for intoxication. Then, only six weeks after arriving in New York, David disappeared from not only the company but also the lives of Eliza and his two children. Eliza was twenty-three years old and suddenly the single mother of two children. History loses track of David Poe after he abandoned his family in New York, but Poe family tradition holds that he died from alcohol abuse within weeks.

For Eliza, there was no time to grieve the end of her marriage. Now solely responsible for the care of two young children, Eliza rejoined the Virginia company in the spring of 1810 and embarked on a southern tour. That December, while on tour in Norfolk, Eliza gave birth to a daughter she named Rosalie. Given the nearly yearlong absence of any records of David Poe, questions remain as to whether David was Rosalie's father. Rumors of Rosalie being the result of an affair between Eliza and another actor have continued, and Edgar himself may have believed this to be true, as several family letters make reference to Rosalie as a "half-sister."

By late January, the Virginia company's southern tour had Eliza back in Charleston accompanied by Edgar and Rosalie. Henry had been left with his grandparents in Baltimore. It had been a long thirteen years since Eliza appeared on a Charleston stage, so most of the public probably did not remember little Miss Arnold from that tumultuous 1797–98 season. Consequently, Alexandre Placide announced Eliza as Mrs. Poe "from the

Boston, New York, and Philadelphia theatres" when she first appeared on January 23 at the Charleston Theatre in the roles of Angela in *The Castle Spectre* and Priscilla Tomboy in *The Romp*.

The 1811 Charleston season saw Eliza in the lead role of Lydia Languish in *The Rivals*, playing opposite John Dwyer, one of the most celebrated actors of the period. Eliza took on several new roles while in Charleston, including Eleanor in *Every One Has His Fault* and Jane in *Wild Oats*, but she also reprised some old, familiar roles like Rosina and Little Pickle. When Eliza was given her benefit night on April 29, three weeks before season's end, she played the leading role of Violante in Susannah Centlivre's *The Wonder*. Along with her busy theater schedule, Eliza also found time to showcase her vocal talents for Charleston, singing in two concerts, including one sponsored by the St. Cecilia Society held at John Sollee's former City Theatre on Church Street.

The nearly four months Eliza spent in Charleston must have been exhausting. Sleepless nights nursing Rosalie and caring for two-year-old Edgar, coupled with her demanding performance schedule, took their toll, and when she returned to Virginia in late May, it was apparent that Eliza was not well. Her appearance had changed, and one reviewer in Norfolk wrote, "Grief may have stolen the roses from her cheeks.…Misfortunes have pressed heavy on her.…She no longer commands that admiration and attention she formerly did."

Unfortunately, it was not grief that gave Eliza her gaunt look but rather some type of infectious fever. The exact nature of Eliza's illness is not known, though historians have diagnosed both tuberculosis and consumption. It is also possible that she was suffering from malaria, then known as ague and fever, which she could have contracted during her stay in Charleston. Whatever the specifics of her illness, Eliza's health quickly began to deteriorate, and when the company returned to the Richmond Theatre in August, Eliza was replaced in her role as Rosina during the season's first week. By mid-October, she stopped appearing on stage completely, and by November, Eliza was bedridden.

On November 29, Eliza's fellow actors gave her a special benefit to raise funds for her care. An appeal appeared in the *Richmond Enquirer* that day, stating, "To the Humane Heart: On this night, Mrs. Poe, lingering on the bed of disease and surrounded by her children, asks your assistance; and asks it perhaps for the last time."

Eliza had no shortage of admirers visit her bedside, and Richmond author Richard Mordecai wrote, "A singular fashion prevails here this season, it is—charity. Mrs. Poe, who you know is a very handsome woman, happens to be very sick, and (having quarreled and parted with her husband) is destitute. The most fashionable place of resort, now is—her chamber—And the skill of cooks and nurses is exerted to procure her delicacies."

Edgar, Henry and Rosalie remained with their mother throughout her illness in Richmond. When she died on December 8, 1811, they were most likely present as well, for Henry, who was then five years old, later recalled his mother's last moments, "[I] heard thy long, thy last farewell."

Upon her death, Edgar received a miniature portrait of his mother and a watercolor she had painted of Boston Harbor in 1808. On the back of the painting she had written, "For my little son Edgar, who should ever love Boston, the place of his birth, and where his mother found her best, and most sympathetic friends."

Eliza Arnold Poe leaned on the charity of strangers one last time when a funeral plot in the graveyard of Richmond's St. John's Church was donated by an admirer. Her grave remained unmarked for more than a century, until a memorial stone was erected in 1927 by the Raven Society of the University of Virginia.

Less than three weeks after Eliza Poe's death, on the day after Christmas, more than six hundred people, including the newly elected governor of Virginia, George W. Smith, packed the Richmond Theatre for a benefit performance for the visiting Alexandre Placide. During the second act of *The Bleeding Nun*, a cry of "The house is on fire!" rang out through the theater. A lit chandelier that had been hoisted in error into some scenery above the stage ignited a fire. Audience members leapt from windows and surged to the only exit door available. Placide wrote from Richmond to the *Charleston Courier* the day after the fire: "We had just time enough to save ourselves, dressed as we were—all the Actors are safe; but alas the Audience suffered beyond the power of language to express. This morning more than one hundred bodies were taken from under the ruins; besides many others, who were severely wounded. Those who perished, are among the most respectable families in this city. I saved nothing. My music, Scenery, Wardrobe, every thing, fell a prey to the flames."

Placide had overestimated the death toll—seventy-seven perished in the fire, including Governor Smith. Anxious to ease any fears of a similar disaster occurring at the Charleston Theatre, Placide wrote a follow-up letter to the *Courier* describing alterations "as will facilitate the escape of the audiences, in case of alarm....Thirteen Doors open into the Street by which the House can be emptied, almost in an instant."

The BURNING of the THEATRE in RICHMOND. VIRGINIA, on the Night of the 26ᵗʰ December 1811, *By which awful Calamity upwards of ONE HUNDRED of its most valuable Citizens suddenly lost their lives and many others were much injured.*

An artist's rendering of the Richmond Theatre fire of December 26, 1811. Ignited during a benefit performance for Charleston's Alexandre Placide, the fire claimed the lives of seventy-seven people, including the governor of Virginia, George W. Smith.

After the fire, a last mention of Edgar Allan Poe's mother by her contemporaries can be found in a statement printed in the *Richmond Enquirer*. Concerned that the public would reject future theatrical performances—with many of the most pious of Richmond's citizens believing the fire to be divine judgment—the statement points to the company's shared grief with the public, while reminding theater patrons of their past charity for the late Eliza Poe: "We are conscious that many have too much cause to wish they had never known us…we have lost our friends, our patrons, our property, and in part our homes.…Never again shall we behold that feminine humanity which so eagerly displayed itself to soothe the victim of disease; and view with exaltation, the benevolent who fostered the fatherless, and shed a ray of comfort to the departed soul of a dying mother."

Eliza Poe played more than three hundred roles in her remarkable career. While the quality and quantity of her stage performances alone certainly merit Eliza a well-deserved place in history, she will always be remembered first as the mother of Edgar Allan Poe. Not even three years old when she passed, Poe was probably too young to have any real memory of her death, but the loss of her still had a profound effect on his psyche and his writing. Poe would spend much of his life searching for

The grave of Edgar Allan Poe's mother, Eliza, at St. John's Church in Richmond, Virginia. *Photo by the author.*

his mother's replacement—first in the maternal and then the romantic feminine. The tragic elements of the premature death of a woman permeate Poe's writing and serve as a recurring theme in some of his most popular poems and short stories.

Edgar Allan Poe remarked later in life that he believed he "owed to his mother every good gift of his intellect or his heart." After the success of "The Raven," Poe gave credit to his mother when he showcased his apparently inherited acting talents while performing popular theatrical readings of his most-famous poem. In an 1845 edition of the *Broadway Journal*, Poe paid tribute to his mother and spoke out against the pious prejudices that still existed against the theater. Those words were added to the back of Eliza Poe's gravestone. He said, "The Actor of talent is poor at heart, indeed, if we do not look with contempt upon the mediocrity even of a king. The writer of this article is himself the son of an actress—has invariably made it his boast—and no earl was ever prouder of his earldom than he of his descent from a woman who, although well born, hesitated not to consecrate to the drama her brief career of genius and of beauty."

2

IN THE ARMY NOW

And so, being young and dipped in folly, I fell in love with melancholy.
—Edgar Allan Poe, "Romance"

While writing my two previous books on the history of piracy in Charleston, I was surprised by how many local pirate legends were shared with me by people who I met. There were wild tales of still-buried treasure on Sullivan's Island and varying accounts of mass pirate hanging sites from White Point Garden to Columbia. There was also a disproportionately large number of Charlestonians who maintained a family tale of having a direct blood relation to one infamous pirate or another. I have lost count of how many great-great-great-great-grandsons and great-great-great-great-granddaughters of Blackbeard and Stede Bonnet I have spoken with.

The same has been true while working on this book about Edgar Allan Poe in Charleston. Just like I found with many of those pirate stories, the majority of the local leads on Poe have proven to be unsubstantiated, but I have still tried to chase down and investigate all but the most outlandish. Most of Poe's connections to Charleston fall into the "Washington slept here" category of history—legend and tradition handed down from generation to generation rather than hard, concrete history. Tangible evidence of Poe's time in Charleston is hard to find and even harder to prove. So, when I was told that Poe had carved his initials into a brick at Fort Moultrie, I was skeptical but still anxious to investigate.

I was told that the initials could be found on a brick near the sally port—the main entrance to the fort. It was late afternoon on a very hot summer day when I went looking for the brick. The fort was already closed for the day when I arrived, but I still had access to the outer walls. I scanned brick by brick around the whole of the sally port and traced my fingers along every crack and groove that I found, hoping to distinguish something that resembled Poe's initials. Those driving by Fort Moultrie must have been confused and a bit alarmed to see a strange man gently rubbing the walls of the fort with one hand while swatting the mosquitos ascending from the tall, wet grass with the other. After perhaps fifteen minutes and about half-a-dozen mosquito bites, my patience was wearing thin, and I was just about to give up when my eye caught an etched brick just to the right of the sally port. Though a deep crack ran through the center, the initials were distinct and unmistakable: EAP. The swooped, rounded *E* and *P* matched those found in Poe's signature. I was excited. As soon as I got home, I reached out to several of my history nerd friends and asked for help finding a solid source who could assist me in authenticating the story. The consensus was that I should speak with Rick Hatcher.

Rick, now retired, worked for the National Park Service for forty years, with more than twenty-two years as a historian for the Fort Sumter National Monument, which includes Fort Moultrie. After chasing him around town for a few days, I was finally able to catch up with him at the Old Exchange and Provost Dungeon in downtown Charleston where he works part-time and continues to pursue his passion for interpreting history. I found Rick stationed in the great hall on the second floor of the exchange, dressed in costume and looking quite refined in his mid-nineteenth century garb. He was sitting behind a table that displayed two muskets and their accoutrements and was answering a barrage of questions from tourists about each musket's range, accuracy and weight. When I sensed a lull in the questioning, I interrupted and introduced myself.

I wanted to sound like a professional historian and not some nut asking about Edgar Allan Poe autographing a two-hundred-year-old fort, so I phrased my question as, "Is the brick and mortar around the sally port of Fort Moultrie original to the fort's construction in the early nineteenth century?" Probably sensing my disappointment in his explanation, Rick gently described that due to the extensive destruction caused by union shells during the Civil War, much of the fort's walls were rebuilt in the decade following the war, including those around the sally port. The sally port itself was also completely rebuilt after the war. Photographs taken shortly after the

The initials E.A.P etched into a brick near Fort Moultrie's sally port. History or hoax? *Photo by the author.*

Union occupation of Charleston at the war's end proved the same. Some Poe fan—or through amazing coincidence, a person with the same initials and handwriting as Poe—had carved into that brick a minimum of sixteen years after Poe's death. It was another dead end for me.

But while the brick turned out to be a dead end, Fort Moultrie is one of our few solid, factual connections to Poe in Charleston. Built on hallowed South Carolina ground on the southern tip of Sullivan's Island, Fort Moultrie was erected on the site of a colonial-era earthen and log fort that helped shape American independence during the Revolutionary War. When a British fleet of warships appeared and "displayed about fifty sail before the town" in June 1776, the fort, then simply known as the Sullivan's Island fort, was only partially completed. Constructed of sand and the spongy wood of the native palmetto tree, it boasted only thirty-one cannons to the British fleet's nearly three hundred. But when Major General Charles Lee, commander of the American forces in the South, asked Colonel William Moultrie, commander of the Sullivan's Island fort, "Do you think you can maintain this post?" Moultrie coolly replied, "Yes, I think I can."

On June 28, the battle began in earnest as the British started the bombardment of the outnumbered Americans in the fort. But in a fun twist of both American military and natural history, the soft, sponge-like wood of the palmetto tree logs that formed the walls of the fort absorbed the impact of the British shot, protecting the Americans and allowing them to return a steady fire into the British warships. So accurate and powerful was the American cannon fire that it literally shot the pants off the British fleet's Commodore Sir Peter Parker, his "Britches…quite torn off, his backside laid bare, his thigh and knee wounded." The Americans were able to disable several ships, and the British withdrew, giving a demoralized America a much-needed win after the recent capture of Boston and defeat at Quebec. The Declaration of Independence would be adopted less than a week later in Philadelphia, and the Sullivan's Island fort was renamed Fort Moultrie in honor of its commander, William Moultrie. South Carolinians celebrate Carolina Day every June 28, and the silent hero, the palmetto tree, is honored on the state flag.

After the war, Fort Moultrie was neglected, and by the early 1790s, little of the fort remained. But when war broke out in 1793 between England and France, Congress, seeking to safeguard the American coast, authorized the first American system of nationwide coastal fortifications. Twenty new forts were built on the Atlantic coast, including a second Fort Moultrie, completed in 1798. A devastating hurricane destroyed this second Fort Moultrie in September 1804. However, when tensions with England put the United States on war footing in 1807, Congress authorized funds for a second American system, and a third Fort Moultrie was completed in early 1809. This third Fort Moultrie is the fort that Edgar Allan Poe would have seen from the deck of the brig *Waltham* when he arrived in Charleston Harbor on November 18, 1827.

But before we discover Poe's history at Fort Moultrie, we need to go back and explore the events that led to his arrival in Charleston. And they start in that bedroom that had become "the most fashionable place of resort" in Richmond where his mother lay dying.

Among those who visited and offered aid to Eliza Poe in her final days was Frances Allan, the wife of Richmond merchant John Allan. The day after Eliza's death, Rosalie was taken in by a Richmond family named Mackenzie, while Edgar's older brother, Henry, was taken in by David Poe's family in Baltimore. The childless Frances Allan was interested in taking three-year-old Edgar into her home. Although initially reluctant, John Allan yielded to his wife's desires and wrote to David Poe's family, detailing the couple's plan for Edgar, promising a liberal education for the middle child. Whether won over by Allan's letter or simply unable to afford both Edgar and Henry in their home, the Poes agreed, and Edgar became the ward of John Allan. Though John Allan would never formally adopt Edgar, the new arrival in the Allan home would take the family name and become Edgar Allan Poe.

Born into a world of art and creativity in the company of poor actors, Poe entered an alternate world with his new Allan family. John Allan, who had emigrated from Scotland in 1795, was a hard-driven, no nonsense, self-made man. Arriving in the United States at only sixteen years old, Allan had taken a job as a clerk in his uncle William Galt's tobacco firm. Allan's uncle was a tough taskmaster and denied his nephew a formal education, giving him instead an on-the-job education. Allan exceled in business, and at the young age of twenty-one, he and a partner, Charles Ellis, formed a firm called the House of Ellis and Allan in Richmond that dealt in tobacco and other various goods and services.

When Poe was six years old, John Allan took the family to England on an extended business trip with the intention of setting up a House of Ellis and Allan in London. The voyage took a miserable thirty-four days, and the family, especially Frances, became very sick. However, upon arriving in London, John Allan told a business associate, "Edgar says Pa say something for me, say I was not afraid coming across the sea."

Poe was enrolled in the Manor House School, a boarding school in London, and the liberal education that John Allan had promised began in earnest. Poe excelled in school, with Allan reporting that the young Edgar was a "good scholar" and read Latin "pretty sharply." But living abroad in London was difficult for the young Poe. Later in life, he recalled this period as "lonely" and "unhappy." Frances Allan, who was almost continually ill with one malady or another throughout the family's time in London, was unable to give the motherly attention and affection Poe craved when he was home during breaks from classes. And John Allan, who fell into financial trouble as the London tobacco market depressed during the family's third year in London, found himself without time for his family, declaring himself "a prisoner in London" and "almost a stranger in my own house." At one point at his boarding school, alone and frightened in an unfamiliar, foreign environment, Poe was shadowed by a cousin who had been directed by the Allan family to ensure he did not try to escape.

In the summer of 1820, John Allan abandoned his hopes of opening his tobacco brokerage house in London and returned to Richmond with the family. Nearly financially ruined, John Allan was forced to move his family into his partner's home. Despite Allan's financial woes, he maintained his commitment to Poe's education, and the eleven-year-old was placed in the academy of a local Latin scholar. His schoolmaster Joseph Clarke reported that Poe "had no love for mathematics" but excelled in poetry. Before Poe turned thirteen, Allan approached Clarke with an unusual question. "Mr. Allan came to me one day with a manuscript volume of verses," Clarke recalled, "which he said Edgar had written, and which the little fellow wanted to have published." Clarke ultimately dissuaded Allan from the poetry's publication, arguing that "Edgar was of a very excitable temperament," and having his verses printed would only serve to swell the preteen's head.

Frances Allan's bouts of illness continued in Richmond, offering her little time for her sensitive young poet, and Poe began looking outside of the Allan household for a maternal figure. When he was fourteen, Poe became infatuated with Jane Stanard, the mother of one of his schoolmates. Poe later described Stanard as "the first, purely ideal love of my soul."

Stanard suffered from mental health issues—depression she described as a "death-like sickness." When she died in April 1824, Poe was devastated and was reported to often be found weeping by Stanard's graveside. A few short verses scratched on a scrap of paper from Allan's desk shortly after Stanard's death by a mourning fifteen-year-old Poe are the first record of his poetry:

> —*Poetry. by. Edgar A. Poe*—
> *Last night with many cares & toils oppress'd*
> *Weary, I laid me on a couch to rest*—

Poe paid a more fitting and eloquent tribute to Stanard seven years later, in 1831, with the poem "To Helen." Poe adopted the name Helen to connect Jane Stanard to Helen of Troy, whose beauty sparked the Trojan War in Homer's *Iliad*.

The poem begins:

> *Helen, thy beauty is to me*
> *Like those Nicean barks of yore,*
> *That gently, o'er perfumed sea,*
> *The weary, way-worn wanderer bore*
> *To his own native shore*

It was around the time of Stanard's death that cracks began to form in John Allan and Poe's relationship. The aspiring poet who wore his heart on his sleeve often found himself at odds with his rigid, business-minded father. John Allan, seemingly unprepared for sharing a home with a moody, sulking teenager, wrote of the rift that was beginning to form: "He does nothing and seems quite miserable, sulky and ill-tempered to all the family." Allan interpreted Poe's attitude as one of thanklessness, stating, "The boy possesses not a spark of affection for us not a particle of gratitude for all my care and kindness towards him." Allan's reminders to Poe of his indebtedness for "a much superior education than ever I received myself" did little to bridge the chasm growing between father and son.

Allan spent the nearly five years since returning to Richmond trying unsuccessfully to settle debts from his failed business venture in London. The House of Ellis and Allan only managed to stay solvent because Allan's uncle William Galt, said to be the richest man in Virginia by this time, bought the assets of the failing business and took on his nearly bankrupt nephew as a secret partner. Allan's business was added to Galt's burgeoning portfolio, which included Galt's own firm, Galt and Galt Junior, real estate in Richmond and Lynchburg, several plantations, a large quantity of stock in the Bank of Virginia and several hundred slaves.

In late March 1825, Allan was having breakfast with his uncle when William Galt, in John Allan's words, "suddenly threw back his head and eyes and seemed oppressed." Uncle Galt died at the breakfast table, and John Allan suddenly found himself rich. Very rich. Allan's share of his uncle's inheritance was estimated at $750,000, and overnight Allan became one of the wealthiest men in Richmond. That summer at public auction, Allan purchased a beautiful two-story home called Moldavia, which was situated on the James River with a view of the capitol building. A contemporary described Moldavia, where the "miserable, sulky and ill-tempered" sixteen-year-old Poe took a room on the second floor, as "more eligible in point of situation perhaps, than any in the city."

Among the Allans' new neighbors was the Royster family. During the summer of 1825, the Roysters' fifteen-year-old daughter Elmira became Poe's first girlfriend. Few details of their relationship exist—only Elmira's recollections much later in life. She did recall of her beau, "He was a beautiful boy—not very talkative…his general manner was sad," and Elmira described the nature of her relationship with Poe as "engaged myself to him." Elmira's parents did not approve of the relationship, likely because of their young ages. Still, an undaunted Poe continued his courtship of Elmira, drawing her likeness in pencil and even introducing Elmira to his brother, Henry, while he was visiting Richmond. That winter, when Edgar was accepted to attend the University of Virginia in Charlottesville, Poe, typical of many young men leaving for college before and since, promised to remain faithful and write unceasingly to his sweetheart in Richmond.

Thomas Jefferson's University of Virginia was only a year old when Poe arrived in February 1826, and it was truly an experiment in education at the time, boasting an entirely elective curriculum and a student self-policed honor code. The result of the latter was an oftentimes chaotic, violent campus. Poe wrote to John Allan of one particularly savage brawl that involved bite wounds: "I saw the whole affair—it took place before my door. I saw the arm afterwards—It was really a serious matter—It was bitten from the shoulder to the elbow—and it is likely that pieces of flesh as large as my hand will be obliged to be cut out."

Like many college students, Poe found himself short of money soon after arriving at university, and within his first week, he wrote Allan asking to send $100. Later in life, Poe stated that Allan sent him to school with exactly $110—just enough to cover tuition. Poe still owed $15 for room rent, $12 for a bed and another $12 for furniture—all of which were due in advance. He also needed to buy books and firewood and make payments to servants for washing clothes and other necessaries. Whether it was a true ignorance of the realities of the life of a university student, as Allan had never attended college, or a willful, active resentment toward Poe, Allan refused to send the needed funds. Poe described that he was "immediately regarded in the light of a beggar" and forced to borrow money "of Jews in Charlottesville at extravagant interest." Poe was even forced to resort to breaking up the furniture in his room for firewood. Desperate and at his wits' end, Poe made the ruinous decision to start gambling to supplement his income. But playing cards was clearly not Poe's forte because when his freshman year ended in December, he was in debt for more than $2,000. His tail between his legs, Poe returned home to Richmond for the Christmas holiday, chased by creditors.

Unfortunately for Poe, back home at Moldavia, the hits just kept coming. On his first night in Richmond, Poe dropped in on a party at the Royster household and was crushed to discover that the festivities were to celebrate Elmira's engagement to another man, Alexander Shelton. Elmira's meddling father had intercepted the letters that Poe sent while away at university, and Elmira, believing that Poe had forgotten her, had become engaged to another man.

Known as the Traylor Miniature, this small watercolor depicts Poe in his late teens. Most scholars agree that the painting is most likely not the result of Poe having sat for the artist during his life but rather an artist's idealized depiction of a young Poe based on other authenticated engravings and paintings. *Courtesy of the Edgar Allan Poe Museum, Richmond, Virginia.*

Heartbroken, miserable and dodging creditors, Poe was becoming difficult to live with, and relations between Poe and John Allan were reaching a boiling point. Allan refused to finance a second term at the University of Virginia, and he refused to offer any assistance settling debts with any of Poe's creditors, though Poe described himself as "every day threatened with a warrant." Allan put a reluctant Poe to work as a clerk in his counting house, but tempers erupted on March 19, 1827, and after a heated argument, Poe essentially ran away from home. That day, Poe sent Allan a message full of moody teen angst. Poe lashed out at Allan, but note that even after all that transpired between father and son regarding finances and debt, Poe still had the nerve to ask Allan to send money:

> *Sir,*
> *After my treatment on yesterday and what passed between us this morning, I can hardly think you will be surprised at the contents of this letter. My determination is at length taken—to leave your house and indeavor* [sic] *to find some place in this wide world, where I will be treated—not as you have treated me…*
>
> *You suffer me to be subjected to the whims & caprice, not only of your white family, but the complete authority of the blacks—these grievances I could not submit to; and I am gone…and if you still have the least affection for me, As the last call I shall make on your bounty, To prevent the fulfillment of the Prediction you this morning expressed, send me as much money as will defray the expences* [sic] *of my passage to some of the Northern cities & then support me for one month, by which time I shall be enabled to place myself some situation where I may not only obtain a livelihood.*

The following day, when Poe had not heard anything from Allan, he sent a follow-up letter just in case Allan had not receive the first:

> *Dear Sir,*
> *….I wrote to you on yesterday explaining my reasons for leaving—I suppose by my not receiving either my trunk, or an answer to my letter, that you did not receive it—I am in the greatest necessity, not having tasted food since Yesterday morning. I have no where* [sic] *to sleep at night, but roam about the Streets—I am nearly exhausted—I beseech you as you wish not your prediction concerning me to be fulfilled—to send me without delay my trunk containing my clothes, and to lend if you will*

not give me as much money as will defray the expence of my passage to Boston ($12,) and a little to support me there until I shall be enabled to engage in some business—I sail on Saturday.

Allan was unimpressed and unmoved by Poe's letters. When Poe did not return home, Allan told his sister that he believed Edgar had "gone to sea to seek his own fortunes." One creditor chasing Poe reported that he had learned that Poe, following in the footsteps of his literary hero Lord Byron, had "gone off entirely, it is said, to join the Greeks" in their fight for independence. There were even rumors circulated that letters written by Poe during his disappearance were postmarked from St. Petersburg in Russia. But the reality was far less exciting and exotic. Poe had gone to Boston and was working as a warehouse clerk under the assumed name of Henri le Rennet, a French corruption of his brother's name Henry Leonard.

Poe, or Henri le Rennet, struggled to make ends meet in Boston, taking a second job at a small newspaper and possibly performing in a Boston theater to supplement his income. He spent any spare time polishing and editing a collection of poetry, some of which had been written when he was only thirteen years old. And somehow, despite the dire state of his finances in Boston, Poe was able to scrounge together enough money to pay a publisher to print fifty copies of a slim book of that poetry, which he titled *Tamerlane and Other Poems*. Unfortunately, this was printed with the author anonymously identified on the title page as "a Bostonian." Debtors' prisons in the United States were still six years from being closed, and Poe, with debts still unsettled in Virginia, did not want to leave a trail for his creditors.

Tamerlane and Other Poems was a collection of ten poems with the central piece being the long-versed "Tamerlane"—a fictionalized deathbed confession of a Persian conqueror of the same name. The volume's poems are rooted in the style and themes of Poe's beloved Romantic writers—youth, love, lost youth, lost love, pride and dreams of what could have been. While *Tamerlane and Other Poems* went seemingly unnoticed by the public—receiving no printed reviews—Poe could declare himself a published writer.

There would be little in the way of time for Poe to enjoy seeing his poetry in print. By the time the fifty copies of *Tamerlane and Other Poems* were offered for sale in Boston bookstores, Poe had already abandoned his Henri le Rennet persona and taken on his next incarnation, enlisting in the United States Army on May 26 under the name of Edgar A. Perry. Poe's choice of "Perry" seems most likely extracted from the headlines of that week's Boston newspapers that were reporting on polar explorer Captain William

Edgar Allan Poe's army enlistment paper. Poe, who was hiding from debt collectors at the time of his enlistment, joined the army under the pseudonym Edgar A. Perry. He also falsely reported that he was twenty-two years old, though he was only eighteen when he joined the army on May 26, 1827. *Courtesy of the National Archives.*

Parry's departure from London aboard the HMS *Hecla*, which was bound for the North Pole. The false name given on his enlistment paper would not be the only misrepresentation. Poe listed his age as twenty-two, though he was only eighteen. One of the few physical descriptions of Poe appears on his enlistment paper: five feet, eight inches tall, fair complexion with brown eyes. Poe listed "clerk" as his occupation.

The image of Poe as a brooding, melancholic writer hunched over a candlelit desk scribbling classic tales of horror makes it difficult to picture him as a prospect for the military, but his decision to join the army may not be as unlikely as it appears. Military service was a proud part of Poe's family history. The grandson of Revolutionary War hero General David Poe Sr., Edgar had shown an interest in his military heritage from an early age. When he was fifteen years old, he became a lieutenant in a volunteer company of boys in Richmond that called themselves the Junior Morgan Riflemen. When Lafayette made a stop in Richmond in 1824—the same tour where he paid tribute to Poe's grandmother—the Junior Morgan Riflemen were appointed to escort Lafayette in his procession through the city. Lafayette proudly reviewed Poe while in his uniform. And there are nonfamilial influences who could have played a role in Poe's decision to join the army. It is certainly possible that Poe may have been inspired to military service simply by his desire to emulate Lord Byron, Poe's beloved warrior poet.

Whatever the reasons, Poe enlisted as a private for a five-year term in the First Regiment of Artillery at a salary of five dollars per month and was assigned to Battery H. Consisting of about fifty men, including twenty-nine other privates, Battery H was commanded by a captain and four lieutenants. Poe spent the summer and early autumn stationed at the regimental headquarters of Fort Independence in Boston Harbor and underwent standard two-month new-recruit training, including infantry drilling; studying of the manual of arms; and learning the proper care, cleaning and firing of artillery pieces.

Five months into his enlistment, on October 31, 1827, Poe's company received orders to sail south to relieve the garrison posted at Fort Moultrie on Sullivan's Island. Just six days later, Poe and the rest of Battery H boarded the brig *Waltham* and sailed for Charleston. A notice from the Boston newspaper *Palladium* was printed in the *Charleston Courier* on November 15, stating, "Boston, November 6. Brig *Waltham*, Webb, for Charleston, dropped down to the Fort Independence, on Sunday, to take on board the garrison, &c. and proceed to Charleston. We learn that she returns to this port with the garrison of that place."

The *Waltham*'s ocean passage from Boston to Charleston proved to be a nightmare. The day after departure, a report filed at Fort Independence noted the weather conditions as "a heavy gale from E.N.E. with some snow and very cold." Gale force winds measure between thirty-nine and fifty-four miles per hour, and one may assume that the report of "a heavy

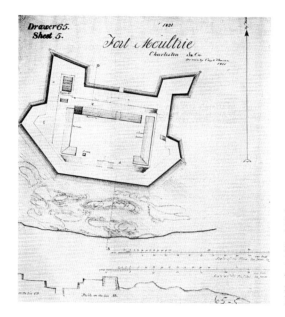

A drawing of Fort Moultrie in 1821 by Captain William T. Poussin shows the fort as it would have appeared when Poe arrived in Charleston on November 18, 1827, as a member of Battery H of the First Regiment of the Artillery.

gale" indicated the high end of the scale. The Beaufort Wind Scale, developed in 1805 by Sir Francis Beaufort of the Royal Navy, gives sea state characteristics defined on an ascending wind speed scale from force zero to force twelve, or from "Calm" to "Hurricane." A strong gale on the Beaufort Wind Scale is considered a force nine, and the seas are described as "high waves (23–32 feet), sea begins to roll, dense streaks of foam, spray may reduce visibility."

Conditions must have been miserable and terrifying onboard the *Waltham*. Most of the soldiers had probably never been to sea, and the sheer terror of a cold, watery grave likely provided the only remedy for their certain seasickness. Poe, who had crossed the Atlantic twice as a child, must have hoped to muster the sea legs and former fortitude that prompted him as a six-year-old to ask John Allan to boast to his colleagues upon the family's arrival in London.

On a coastal passage like that of the *Waltham*, the dangers of a lee shore would have posed the greatest risk to a vessel. The strong east-north-easterly wind encountered by the *Waltham* would have only exponentially increased that danger, and the *Waltham*'s captain would have been obliged to stand far out to sea to avoid the perils of the coast. The day after the *Waltham*'s departure from Fort Independence, a vessel named the *Aurora* fell victim to those same strong onshore winds and was driven onto a shoal, sinking just off Boston.

The *Waltham*'s passage from Boston to Charleston took nearly two agonizing weeks, but to the great relief of Poe and the other members of Battery H, the *Waltham* came "in full view of the low coast of South Carolina" and anchored in Charleston Harbor on Sunday, November 18. Another vessel, named *Romulus*, which had departed Boston in convoy with the *Waltham*, was feared to have sunk until its arrival at Charleston three days later.

A report in the *Courier* on November 19 recorded:

> *Arrived Yesterday*
> *Brig Waltham, Webb, Boston 11 days. With a company of U.S. Troops for the Garrison at Fort Moultrie. Passengers, Lieut. H.W. Griswold, U.S.A., Lady and child, Lieut. J. Howard, U.S.A., Lady and three children, and Dr. J. Dodd, U.S.A.*

Evidence of the perils of the passage to Charleston are reflected in a letter printed in the *Courier* the day of the *Waltham*'s arrival. Signed by several of Poe's commanding officers, the letter heaps praise and gratitude on the *Waltham*'s captain, George Webb:

> *A Card—Fort Moultrie, Charleston Harbor, S.C., November 18th, 1827. The undersigned officers of the 1st Regiment of Artillery, in behalf of ourselves, families, and a detachment of men, tender to Captain George Webb, our most unfeigned thanks, for his kind attention to us while on board the Brig Waltham, on her passage from the harbor of Boston to Charleston, South Carolina; more especially for his nautical abilities, under Divine Providence, in extricating the vessel under his command, from most imminent danger, when drifting on a lee shore, off the shoals of Cape Cod, as well as good management during several severe gales of wind, while on our passage.*

After their unnerving and inauspicious arrival to Charleston, the members of Battery H quickly settled into a sedentary life at their new post at Fort Moultrie. Poe had the good fortune to enlist during a period in U.S. military history referred to as the Thirty Years' Peace. Encompassing the three decades following the War of 1812, this unprecedented period of peace would only be interrupted by the Seminole Wars in Florida. (Ten years after Poe's arrival at the fort, Seminole leader Osceola, who was captured during the second Seminole War, was imprisoned at Fort Moultrie in 1837. He would die of a throat infection only a few months after his arrival. His grave stands just outside the fort's walls near the sally port.)

Military life during the Thirty Years' Peace consisted mostly of drilling and housekeeping. The typical orders for the day for the garrison at Fort Moultrie, as described by Charleston author Hervey Allen in his Poe biography *Israfel: The Life and Times of Edgar Allan Poe*, brimmed with routine and tedium: "The garrison rose about five-thirty a.m., policed, breakfasted, and engaged in a short morning's drill, varied from time to time by exercises at the great guns. The passage of time was punctuated by the sharp reports of the sunrise and sunset guns, the strains of the bugles at meal times and retreat, and by nothing more."

The newly arrived recruits of Battery H would have found space tight at their new home in the fort's stone walls—the interior of the fort measures only four hundred feet at its widest point. Poe's new home was in the enlisted men's barracks, which formed the western flank of a three-sided, horseshoe-shaped configuration of buildings. The officer's barracks stood opposite the enlisted men's, separated by a small parade ground. Only the top floor of the fort's barracks buildings served as living quarters, as the hot, damp lower rooms were deemed uninhabitable and used only for kitchens, messes and storerooms. Due to the cramped and uncomfortable quarters, some senior staffers were permitted to live outside of the fort in civilian houses in the nearby village of Moultrieville, which had only been incorporated ten years earlier, in 1817, and was beginning to grow as a summertime resort town for Charlestonians. During the last month of Poe's posting at Fort Moultrie, in November 1828, funds were secured from Washington to overhaul the dilapidated dwellings in the fort. The barracks were enlarged with piazzas added to the second floors, and to make conditions more tolerable in the summer heat, the outer walls of all the buildings and parapets were painted yellow to reflect the scorching rays of the sun.

The six-sided fort, completed in 1809 under the supervision of Captain Alexander Macomb of the U.S. Corps of Engineers, was designed and built entirely to support its role as a seashore battery meant to shell any enemy vessels attempting to enter Charleston Harbor via the main channel. The fort's ramparts were fifteen feet high, packed with sand between triple courses of heavy brick and topped around the outer edges by granite coping stones. Though it would never boast as many during peacetime, the fort could mount nearly fifty large artillery pieces *en barbette*—a French military expression meaning only the barrel of the fort's big guns protruded above its parapets, allowing gun crews to load and fire artillery pieces from

The interior of Fort Moultrie. The enlisted men's barracks were razed by the Confederates in 1863 to eliminate the danger of flying debris in the event of enemy shelling. A long, rectangular brick foundation is all that remains to mark the location of the two-story brick building that Poe would have called home while stationed at the fort. Behind the brick foundation, the fort's original 1809 powder magazine and its protective brick wall, called a traverse, still stand. *Photo by Jennifer Taylor.*

behind the relative protection of the fort's walls. The main gunpowder magazine was tucked in the rear of the fort behind the enlisted men's quarters, with several smaller magazines scattered around the fort for ease of access during times of combat.

Poe, despite joining under false pretenses, thrived and prospered under the discipline of army life, particularly during his posting at Fort Moultrie. The army curiously proved to be the only institution to support and appreciate Poe's talents during his lifetime. Being educated and literate—probably unlike most of the other new recruits of Battery H—Poe was promoted to company clerk by his commanding officer, Lieutenant Joshua Howard. In this capacity, Poe traded some of the more mundane tasks, such as guard duty, for responsibilities like filling out monthly reports and managing payroll. He also served as assistant to the assistant commissary of subsistence—an officer responsible for the management of the garrison's food supplies.

On May 1, Poe continued his rise through the ranks and doubled his salary to ten dollars per month when he was promoted to artificer, a more mechanically inclined position responsible for the delicate job of measuring gunpowder and preparing munitions. His success as a soldier is evidenced in his commanding officers' glowing reviews, including, "He at once performed the duties of company clerk and assistant in the Subsistent Department, both of which duties were promptly and faithfully done," and "he has been exemplary in his deportment, prompt and faithful in the discharge of his duties—and is high worthy of confidence."

But despite his promotions and endorsements, Poe decided not long after his arrival at Fort Moultrie that army life did not suit him and began looking for a way out of his enlistment. He determined that a hardship discharge was the most tenable, but he recognized that managing to receive any type of discharge was not going to be easy. First, Poe had signed a five-year enlistment, and when he arrived in Charleston, he had only served for six months. Second, and more confoundingly, a hardship discharge meant that he would have to share the details of his perceived hardships, which would entail coming clean to the army about his identity, age and past.

Fortunately, Poe had the good fortune of finding a sympathetic ear in Lieutenant Joshua Howard, and he disclosed to Howard his real name and age and explained the circumstances that led him to enlist in the army. Howard, who Poe later described as a fatherly figure who acted from the "goodness of his heart" and "has always been kind to me," was sympathetic to Poe's plight and agreed to help. But the terms of Howard's assistance in procuring a discharge required the seemingly impossible—because of his young age, Poe would have to make amends with John Allan and receive his blessing to leave the army.

Howard made the first foray toward reconciliation between Poe and John Allan, writing a letter to Allan that explained Poe's desire to restore relations with his father and hope for Allan's blessing for a discharge from the army. The letter from Howard was probably the first news Allan had received of Poe's whereabouts since he had stormed out of the house in March of the previous year. But news of his wayward son did not strike a note of sentimentality, and his reply to Howard was cold and disappointing, although probably not totally unexpected. Allan wrote, "He had better remain as he is until the termination of his enlistment."

On December 1, 1828, just after Battery H received orders from regimental headquarters to sail from Fort Moultrie to Fort Monroe in Virginia, Poe wrote to his father, hoping Allan had a change of heart:

I have been in the American army as long as suits my ends or my inclination, and it is now time that I should leave it—To this effect I made known my circumstances to Lieut Howard who promised me my discharge solely upon a re-conciliation with yourself—He insisted upon my writing you & that if a re-conciliation could be effected he would grant me my wish…He has always been kind to me, and, in many respects, reminds me forcibly of yourself.

The period of an Enlistment is five years—the prime of my life would be wasted—I shall be driven to more decided measures if you refuse to assist me.

A letter addressed to Lieut: J. Howard assuring him of your reconciliation with myself (which you have never yet refused) & desiring my discharge would be all that is necessary.

On December 4, the transport vessel *Harriet* arrived at Charleston with "two companies of U.S. Troops, under the command of Capt. Belton" to relieve the garrison at Fort Sumter. The *Harriet* cleared the day after its arrival and rested at anchor for one week before making the transfer of troops at the fort. On December 11, with Poe and the rest of Battery H onboard, the *Harriet* went to sea for Norfolk.

As the *Harriet* slipped out of Charleston Harbor, its wake washed over the sands of an undeveloped sliver of land extending from James Island where another masonry fort would be built and garrisoned by soldiers just like those departing. Only a few days before the *Harriet* sailed, Congress had approved funding for a "pentagonal, three-tiered, masonry fort with truncated angles." The fort, for which construction plans had been drafted the previous year, would be named Fort Sumter. More than thirty-two years later, construction of Fort Sumter would still not be completed when the first shots of the Civil War were fired at its walls.

As Poe stood among the other members of Battery H on the crowded deck of the *Harriet*, watching Fort Moultrie and his former island home dip beneath the horizon, he likely recollected the literal and figurative storms that had chased him to Charleston more than one year earlier onboard the *Waltham*. After so much time and distance, he must

John Allan.

55

have concluded that his circumstances were not much improved. Poe was still at odds with and estranged from John Allan, with whom he needed to reconcile to have any hope of escaping from the three and a half years remaining in his enlistment. And the army, which had so far served as a place to hide, was now, by sending him to his new post at Fort Monroe in Virginia, placing Poe perilously close to the debt collectors who he had managed to dodge for the two previous years.

Adding insult to injury, on the same day the *Harriet* sailed from Charleston Harbor, Poe's first girlfriend, Elmira Royster, was marrying Alexander Shelton four hundred miles away in Richmond. If Poe could find any solace as the *Harriet* steered north, it was that unlike the *Waltham*'s storm-tossed voyage thirteen months earlier, the passage from Charleston to Fort Monroe would prove uneventful, riding the warm water currents of the Gulf Stream and arriving in Norfolk, Virginia, after only four days at sea.

On December 22, the *Gazette* in Charleston listed the following notice from a correspondent: "Norfolk, December 15: The ship *Harriet*, Johnson, fm Charleston, with two companies of U.S. Artillery, anchored off Old Point this afternoon."

Poe had spent just short of thirteen months in Charleston. To say that tracing and documenting Poe's time while stationed at Fort Moultrie is a challenge would be an understatement. In fact, there is more evidence of Poe's four-month stay in Charleston as a two-year-old than there is of his more than one-year stay while in the army. The challenge is in no small measure because throughout his life, Poe himself deliberately tried to hide his stint in the army. Poe remained resolutely elusive in interviews and biographical sketches about his army years, and he seemed more than happy to perpetuate the false narratives of his rumored adventures abroad in Greece and Russia. So complete was his cover-up that Poe's thirteen months stationed at Fort Moultrie went undetected until 1885—thirty-six years after his death—when it was discovered by George E. Woodberry while he was researching for a biography of Poe for Houghton Mifflin's *American Men of Letters*.

While the specifics of Poe's experiences in the Lowcountry are elusive and accurately described by Hervey Allen as "oblivion has it in its quiet keeping…a whole year whose social and whose human contacts are nearly blank," there are some reasonable assumptions that can be made about Poe's time stationed at Fort Moultrie. First, it does not require too much detective work to conclude that Poe, like any other soldier stationed at the fort, anxiously took advantage of any leave time allowed to escape the remoteness of his island home and make the short trip across the harbor into the relative bustle of the city of Charleston. As Hervey Allen describes, "Leave in Charleston was the only relaxation of the garrison." Poe's own recollection of Sullivan's Island reveals the stark impression the island made: "Near the western extremity, where Fort Moultrie stands, and where are some miserable frame buildings, tenanted, during the summer, by the fugitives from Charleston dust and fever, may be found." Aside from swimming and beachcombing, Sullivan's Island had little to offer a young man in terms of recreation and entertainment in 1828. And while Poe was a surprisingly strong swimmer—famously swimming more than seven miles on the James River near Richmond when he was fifteen years old—and he did seem to have an interest in seashells, editing a book on conchology in 1839, the only hobby or avocation that we can be certain Poe pursued during his free time while stationed at Fort Moultrie was, of course, writing. Unfortunately, Poe's discretion regarding his identity during his enlistment means that crediting or linking any published works directly to Poe is impossible. There are no poems, stories or essays signed by Edgar Allan Poe, or even Edgar A. Perry, published during the period Poe spent in the Lowcountry.

It is possible, and perhaps even likely, that Poe sent submissions either anonymously or signed under a pseudonym to one or more of Charleston's many newspapers or magazines. Hugh Swinton Legare's *Southern Review*, the South's first serious literary magazine, saw its first issue published in Charleston shortly after Poe's arrival at Fort Moultrie. Legare's journal seems one of the more likely candidates to have received a submission from Poe, but the essays published in the *Southern Review* are for the most part unsigned and their authors remain unknown today.

There is some evidence that works produced during Poe's time in the army may have been surreptitiously published under his brother Henry's name. Henry managed to have some of his poetry published in a short-lived magazine called *North American*, and two poems submitted by Henry, signed under the byline of W.H.P., bear striking similarities to his brother's style and form. There is also a brief piece of prose titled "A Fragment" signed under W.H.P. that was unlike any of Henry's other writing and may belong to Edgar as well. "A Fragment," a first-hand account by a desperate man about to shoot himself, is told by a mad, insistent narrator—a style that would become a standard of Edgar's later work.

But while this is purely speculative, in late 1829, Poe did manage to publish a book of poetry titled *Al Aaraaf, Tamerlane, and Minor Poems*, which contains verses that were most certainly written by Poe while stationed at Fort Moultrie. The book of poetry included overhauled versions of several of the poems from Poe's first volume, including "Tamerlane," but the centerpiece was an epic-style poem named "Al Aaraaf." Poe considered *Al Aaraaf, Tamerlane, and Minor Poems* to be his first published work, with the title page identifying the author as Edgar A. Poe, rather than the anonymous "A Bostonian" in his previous publication.

Sadly, this freedom to use his own name would come only after more personal tragedy and loss. Two months after arriving at Fort Monroe, Poe received word that his mother had become desperately ill. When Frances Allan died on February 28 from what a Richmond newspaper described as "lingering and painful" sickness, a devastated Poe was only able to arrive home on furlough the day after his mother's burial at Shockoe Hill Cemetery—the same cemetery that held the grave of Jane Stanard. Poe wrote of his mother's death, "I have had a fearful warning & have hardly known before what distress was." The cycle of the loss and longing for a maternal figure for Poe reengaged.

Frances Allan's passing did force a reunion, albeit a somber one, between Poe and his estranged father. The death of his wife had softened John Allan, and after nearly two years without seeing one another, Allan and Poe were able to draw a temporary truce from their shared grief. Poe, who by this time had been promoted to the rank of sergeant major—the highest rank possible for noncommissioned officers—had decided on a new plan for his life and asked Allan for his assistance in pursuing the "direction my 'future views & expectations' were inclined." Contrary to his letter from Fort Moultrie only a few months earlier, where he stated that he had served in the military "as long as suits my ends or my inclination," Poe now desired to attend the United States Military Academy at West Point and make a career out of the army. Allan endorsed the plan, and Poe returned to Fort Monroe with the long-coveted letter of reconciliation from Allan giving his blessing for Poe's discharge. Curiously, even with the required letter in hand, Poe still chose to be deceptive with the army to the very end. In the letter that Poe's commanding officer at Fort Monroe, Colonel House, sent to general command in New York requesting Poe's discharge, there are false statements that Poe clearly represented to garner sympathy and hedge his bets on procuring his hardship discharge. Poe falsely placed both of his parents in the deadly Richmond Theatre fire of 1809. Poe's commanding officer's letter requesting a discharge begins, "GENERAL, I request your permission to discharge from the service Edgar A. Perry, at present the Sergeant-Major of the 1st Reg't of Artillery.…The said Perry is one of a family of orphans whose unfortunate parents were the victims of the conflagration of the Richmond theatre, in 1809."

On April 15, 1829, under Special Order No. 28, Sergeant Major Edgar A. Perry was discharged from the army, contingent upon the securing of a substitute. On April 17, in exchange for a promised seventy-five dollars from Poe, Sergeant Samuel "Bully" Graves "re-enlisted substitute for Sgt. Major Perry."

Upon his discharge, Poe moved in with family in Baltimore, and while he waited for a response to his West Point application, he passed the summer editing and polishing those poems that would appear in *Al Aaraaf, Tamerlane, and Minor Poems*. That autumn, with funding from John Allan, Poe managed to have 250 copies of the seventy-one page *Al Aaraaf, Tamerlane, and Minor Poems* printed by the Baltimore publishing firm of Hatch and Dunning. Copies first appeared in bookstores in December 1829. Unlike his 1827 *Tamerlane and Other Poems*, Poe's newest book of poetry did receive reviews in several publications in Baltimore and Boston, with critics focusing on the volume's central piece, the long and complicated "Al Aaraaf." Unfortunately for Poe, most of those reviews were not kind. Critics seized on the sheer overwhelming size of "Al Aaraaf," Poe's longest poem by far, and its obscure complicated references. One critic described "Al Aaraaf" as "a pile of brick-bats," while another review pointed to the poem's confusing form and text, stating, "All our brain-cudgelling [*sic*] could not compel us to understand it." One particularly savage reviewer for the *Baltimore Minerva and Emerald* asked, "Has the poet been struck dumb with palsy?"

The epic poem is inspired by the Islamic concept of *Al Aaraaf*, a wall between paradise and hell depicted in the Koran where, much like purgatory, souls that are neither necessarily good nor particularly bad must stay until judgment by God and entry into paradise. Poe brackets theology with science, placing Al Aaraaf on a rare star discovered in 1572 by Tycho Brahe that only stayed visible for sixteen months before fading away. The poem's many obscure and technical references obligated Poe to add nearly as many lines of footnotes as poetic verse.

The poem carries a dream-like, mystic mood but its uneven and straying architecture makes following the poem's rhythm and direction difficult. Some of these confusing lines include:

> *She ceas'd—and buried then her burning cheek*
> *Abash'd, amid the lilies there, to seek*
> *A shelter from the fervor of His eye;*

For the stars trembled at the Deity.
She stirr'd not—breath'd not—for a voice was there
How solemnly pervading the calm air!
A sound of silence on the startled ear
Which dreamy poets name "the music of the sphere."

It is not an easy read. I count myself, at best, an amateur when it comes to interpreting, appraising or even appreciating poetry; however, even a novice like myself can recognize that any poem that requires near-constant references to footnotes has some fundamental flaws. While working on this book, I read a lot of Poe, and I mean *a lot* of Poe, and I can report that I will be perfectly content if I never read "Al Aaraaf" again.

Some scholars chalk up the failings of "Al Aaraaf" to a sophomoric slump. In my opinion, the poem seems simply a case of Poe biting off more than he could chew—the over-reaching of an ambitious twenty-year-old. Poe himself commented that the poem contained "much extravagance which I have not had time to throw away." And for his part, Poe did seem to learn some lessons from the backlash against "Al Aaraaf," specifically in the importance of brevity, for his future poetry. "Al Aaraaf" served as the inspiration for one of the key principles found in his later work, "The Poetic Principle," in which he lays out the rules that make for a good poem, railing against long, epic poems, stating, "If, at any time, any very long poems were popular in reality—which I doubt—it is clear that no very long poem will ever be popular again."

THAT DURING HIS MORE than one year at Fort Moultrie, Poe was writing prolonged, mystical poetry about a star and its connection to theological principles found in the Koran is odd and unexpected. Frankly, it is a little disappointing. Poe's more than one year stationed at Fort Moultrie surely offered more than enough beauty and inspiration to write boundless verses about the Lowcountry's landscape, history, legends and lore. So, what happened? I take this occasion to remind you of the age-old adage "good things come to those who wait." Those impressions and inspirations of the Lowcountry were in Poe's head and in his heart. He had just hidden them away like he had hidden his identity. But they would find their way into his work—it just took fifteen years. And when they did appear, those impressions and inspirations generated a profound, career-defining story that was unlike any other that Poe would write.

3

A Bug, a Box and a Balloon

A feeling, for which I have no name, has taken possession of my soul—a
sensation which will admit of no analysis, to which the lessons of by-gone time
are inadequate, and for which I fear futurity itself will offer me no key.
—Edgar Allan Poe, "MS. Found in a Bottle"

In 1839, a thirty-year-old Edgar Allan Poe was consumed by puzzles. Cryptography, the art of writing and solving codes, had become widely popular in America, and Poe had declared himself a master of the science. "Nothing intelligible can be written which, with time, I cannot decipher," Poe wrote in a letter to a friend. While working as the editor of Philadelphia's *Burton's Gentleman Magazine* in the autumn of 1839, Poe had taken up a side job doing anonymous hackwork for *Alexander's Weekly Messenger*, self-described as "the largest and cheapest family newspaper in the world." It would be within *Alexander's* pages that Poe would first show off his puzzle-solving prowess, challenging readers to stump him with substitution ciphers—secret messages encoded into alternate letters, numbers or symbols. Poe goaded his readers, "We pledge ourselves to read it forthwith however unusual or arbitrary may be the character employed."

Readers overwhelmingly responded to the challenge, and over the next six months, Poe solved more than one hundred submitted cryptograms. But the flood of puzzles eventually grew too much even for Poe, and he wrote mockingly in a column in *Alexander's*, "Do people really think that we have nothing in the world to do but read hieroglyphics?" In April 1840,

Poe solved his last cryptogram at *Alexander's*, which had been sent in by a seventeen-year-old Schuyler Colfax, who, three decades later, would become vice-president under Ulysses S. Grant. Poe quit his side gig at *Alexander's* a month later and temporarily put his puzzle-solving days aside.

It was around the time that he was solving his last cryptogram at *Alexander's* that Poe learned that William Burton was planning to sell his *Gentleman's Magazine*. In reaction, Poe turned to self-preservation and quickly began to circulate a prospectus for his own magazine to be named *Penn Magazine* that he promised to be free of "any tincture of the buffoonery, scurrility, or profanity." When Burton heard of Poe's plan to start a rival publication, he, of course, fired Poe on the spot. And though a cocky Poe wrote to a contributor, "You wish to know my prospects with the *Penn*? They are glorious," he spent much of 1840 postponing the launch due to insufficient funding. A run on banks in February 1841 sent business credit crashing and abruptly and definitively ended *Penn*'s prospects before Poe could even print the first issue. Luckily, he did receive a lifeline just a few weeks later when George Rex Graham, who had bought William Burton's magazine for $3,500, brought Poe back as editor of the newly dubbed *Graham's Lady's and Gentleman's Magazine*.

Poe's tenures at *Burton's*, *Alexander's* and *Graham's* were just a few of the postings in the roller-coaster professional career that was most associated with Poe during his lifetime—that of an editor. The swift falls, and often even swifter rebounds, of his editorial career, like those at *Burton's* and *Graham's*, were common hallmarks of that career, as were the dashed and unrealized dreams of the publication of his own literary magazine. Poe attempted a failed relaunch of *Penn* two years later under a new name, *Stylus*.

Poe's abrasive personality, self-serving motives and growing penchant for alcohol, which made him prone to turning moody, disagreeable and argumentative, meant that he was not employed for long by any one publication. A colleague at his first editorial position recalled, "Mr. Poe was a fine gentleman when he was sober....But when he was drinking he was about one of the most disagreeable men I have ever met." Poe's genetic disposition to alcoholism, which he referred to as his "illness," haunted him throughout his life, even potentially lending to his death. His brother, Henry, who also fell victim to the family curse, was characterized by Edgar as "entirely given up to drink" in the months before Henry's death on August 1, 1831, of what was described as "intemperance."

When Poe did manage to stay sober and gainfully employed, he worked doggedly as an editor, particularly as a reviewer of poetry and prose, famously building a reputation as a meticulous, merciless, take-no-prisoners critic, which earned him the nickname the Tomahawk Man. Poe wrote, "In criticism, I will be bold, and as sternly, absolutely just with friend and foe. From this purpose nothing shall turn me." Poe made more than a few enemies through his biting criticisms in which he called out the perceived shortcomings of authors, ranging from flimsy plotlines and themes to poor grammar, skewering their work with criticisms like "despicable in every respect," "unworthy of a schoolboy" and, my personal favorite, "The most remarkable feature in this production is the bad paper on which it is printed."

Poe's editorial career and subsequent reputation as a vicious critic was kickstarted in June 1833 when Baltimore's *Saturday Visiter* announced a contest with "a premium of 50 dollars for the best Tale." An ambitious Poe submitted an entire collection of stories, and the judges singled out his tale of a shipwrecked man's voyage on a ghost ship, "MS. Found in a Bottle," as the winner. One of the contest's judges, southern novelist John Pendleton Kennedy, took a keen interest in Poe and encouraged him to submit further stories to his friend Thomas W. White, whose new literary paper titled the *Southern Literary Messenger* was just publishing its first edition in Richmond. Kennedy followed up on Poe's submissions to the *Messenger* with a personal letter to White, hinting at hiring Poe: "He is very clever with his pen—classical and scholar-like. He wants experience and direction, but I have no doubt he can be made very useful to you." White was impressed by the two stories that Poe submitted, "Berenice" and "Morella," and in August 1835, White hired him as an assistant editor of the *Messenger*.

Poe's hiring at the *Messenger* proved timely, as the second-most mysterious event of his life, after his unexplained death, occurred on May 16, 1836, when he married his thirteen-year-old cousin Virginia Clemm. Poe's marriage to Virginia raised more than a few eyebrows before the ink had even dried on the couple's marriage license, which falsely reported Virginia's age as "of the full age of twenty-one years," and the scandalous nature of the union has not aged well over the last two centuries. I admit that the marriage is, at the minimum, a little *disturbing*—especially when viewed through a twenty-first-century lens. The fact that Poe first met Virginia in Baltimore during the summer of 1829, when she was only seven years old, while he was awaiting news from West Point, and that Poe referred to his bride-to-be as "Sissy" makes the marriage even more uncomfortable. But a little context does feather the edges of the creepy factor, at least a little.

This post-mortem portrait of Virginia Clemm Poe was said to have been commissioned in the hours immediately following her death from tuberculosis on January 30, 1847, when it was realized that no portrait of her in life existed.

First, there is evidence that the marriage was—at least in the first couple of years—platonic. Poe reportedly said that for two years he occupied a room alone and did not "assume the position of husband." Further, Poe's marriage seems to be nearly as much about Virginia's mother (Poe's aunt), Maria Clemm, as it was about Virginia herself. Maria Clemm, affectionately called "Muddy," had assumed the maternal role in Poe's life after his discharge from the army, filling the void left after the death of Frances Allan. In the years immediately following his stint as an enlisted man, Poe had lived with Virginia and Maria in Baltimore, and the trio had formed, at least in Poe's mind, the affectionate and nurturing—albeit unorthodox—family that Poe had longed for his whole life.

Poe received a letter from Maria a few weeks after his arrival at his new post at the *Messenger*. Maria sought his advice about an invitation extended to her by cousin Neilson Poe to take in Virginia and educate her and perhaps take in Maria as well. Poe panicked at what he perceived to be the certain loss of his little family. From Poe's perspective, a quick marriage to Virginia would curb this threat and consolidate his unusual family unit. He wrote to Maria in hysterics, "I am blinded by tears while writing thi[s] letter....I love, you know I love Virginia passionately devotedly. I cannot express in words the fervent devotion I feel towards my dear little cousin....Oh God have mercy on me!...Oh, Aunty, Aunty you loved me once—how can you be so cruel now?" Poe even hinted at suicide if faced with losing Maria and Virginia and having to exist alone again, stating, "My last my last my only hold on life is cruelly torn away, I have no desire to live and will not."

It is probably fair to say that a psychiatrist could have made an entire career out of trying to unriddle Poe, particularly in the dynamics of his marriage to Virginia and its relationship with his protracted maternal absence. But Poe offers perhaps the best insight into the subject in his poem "To My Mother." Written for and about Maria Clemm and published only a few months before Poe's death in 1849, "To My Mother" beautifully relates the influence and strange, complicated role of Maria Clemm in Poe's life:

> *My mother—my own mother, who died early,*
> *Was but the mother of myself; but you*
> *Are mother to the one I loved so dearly,*
> *And thus are dearer than the mother I knew*
> *By that infinity with which my wife*
> *Was dearer to my soul than its soul-life.*

Poe's proposal of marriage to Virginia may also have been motivated by factors even less romantic than those of securing a surrogate mother in Maria Clemm. The marriage may have been grounded, at least partially, in the prospect of financial gains. By wedding a cousin on his father's side and subsequently becoming the beneficiary of Virginia's mother, Poe may have hoped to improve his chances of receiving a share of his late grandfather's $240 annual pension. The state of Maryland had been paying out General Poe's pension to his widow, Elizabeth, since his death in 1816. When Elizabeth died in 1835, Poe may have hoped to have access to any portion of that pension that may have come to Maria Clemm. Marrying under the pretext of gaining some portion of the relatively paltry sum of $240 per year is not as ridiculous as it may first appear, as at the time of his nuptials, Poe was desperately poor. In the letter to Thomas White, in which John Pendleton Kennedy encouraged White to hire Poe as an editor at the *Southern Literary Messenger*, Kennedy concluded with a description of Poe, writing "And, poor fellow! He is very poor."

Poe's state of destitution at the time of his nuptials was not without irony, as he could have been, and in his opinion *should* have been, abundantly wealthy by 1835. When John Allan died on March 27, 1834, Poe estimated his father's worth at $750,000, of which even a small portion could have secured him financially for the rest of his life. But when Allan's last will and testament was

Poe's aunt and, after marrying his cousin Virginia, mother-in-law, Maria "Muddy" Clemm.

read, Poe received absolutely nothing. There was not even a mention of the name Edgar Allan Poe in Allan's will. It was as if for John Allan, Poe had never existed. And after Frances Allan's death, in many ways, he did stop existing to John Allan.

After his discharge from the army in 1829, Poe's "future views & expectations" of graduating from West Point and becoming a career army officer proved short lived. He did get accepted to West Point, and he reported for duty that June, but another fracture in Poe and John Allan's relationship curtailed his plans. This time, the rift formed after the revelation that John Allan had fathered illegitimate twins while married to Frances. Poe was devastated by the news and resented Allan for his infidelity. When Allan married—too quickly in Poe's opinion—Louisa Gabriella Patterson in the autumn of 1830, Poe's perception of Allan's betrayal of his late mother only grew and festered.

Further straining the relationship, Poe began to rightfully sense that Allan's new family, and two potential new heirs, were squeezing him out of John Allan's attentions and, more importantly, his finances. Tensions grew heated in letters exchanged with Allan while Poe was at West Point, and Poe lashed out at Allan, adducing his late mother's solitary love for him:

"If she had not have died while I was away there would have been nothing for me to regret—Your love I never valued—but she I believed loved me as her own child."

Matters only got worse when Poe's army substitute, Samuel "Bully" Graves, came dunning for the still unpaid seventy-five dollars Poe had promised. Poe wrote to Graves explaining that he had tried to get the money from his father, but Allan "always shuffles me off," and he added the fateful line, "Mr. A is not very often sober." Somehow, this letter became known to Allan, and it proved to be the veritable last straw. Much like he had done while Poe was attending the University of Virginia, Allan withheld necessary funding from Poe while at West Point, leaving an anxious Poe teetering at the brink of penury—by the year's end Poe had a balance of just twenty-four cents.

But Poe would not stand for Allan's abuses this time, and he retaliated, writing, "From the time of writing this I shall neglect my studies and duties at the institution.…I should subject myself to dismission." True to his word, Poe skipped evening parades, class parades, church, reveille roll calls and guard duties until he was court martialed on January 28 for "Neglect of his Academic duties." Poe was found guilty on all charges, and the court passed judgment "that the cadet EA Poe be dismissed from the service of the United States." Poe did not even complete one full year at West Point.

Poe remained estranged from Allan for the next three years. The pair did exchange some letters, mostly sent by Poe and mostly containing requests to send money to pay for one debt or another. Allan generally ignored Poe's requests, or if he did send money, it was only a fraction of the amount Poe requested. Whether the two ever met in person again after Poe's dismissal from West Point is still debated. A secondhand account did emerge years later, relating that upon hearing of Allan's ill health in 1834, Poe had traveled to Richmond to see his father one last time. Reportedly, upon Poe's arrival at Moldavia, Allan's wife tried to prevent Poe from going upstairs to Allan's sickroom, but Poe rushed past her. When Poe entered the room, Allan, who by this time suffered so badly from dropsy that he could not lie down and was confined to an armchair, raised his cane as if to strike Poe and ordered him to leave. On March 27, 1834, only a few weeks after this possible last encounter, Allan's wife found her husband dead, sitting alone in his armchair.

When Poe moved back to Richmond in 1835 to work at the *Southern Literary Messenger*, he lived in a boardinghouse owned by Martha Yarrington, located on Broad Street near Richmond's Capitol Square. Poe's new residence was quite sparse compared to the grandeur of his boyhood home at Moldavia, situated only a few blocks away. Following his unusual wedding, also performed at Mrs. Yarrington's boardinghouse, Poe's quarters became even more cramped as he began sharing his home with both Virginia and Maria Clemm. He remained in Richmond at the *Messenger* until early 1837 but managed during his sixteen-month tenure to be fired, rehired and then fired again by Thomas White for his drinking and sometimes overtly scathing reviews that White viewed as bordering on libel. Though Poe proclaimed that circulation of the *Messenger* more than quadrupled while he served as editor, White spoke caustically of Poe after firing him, stating that the *Messenger* would "outlive all the injury it has sustained from Mr. Poe's management" and concluding of Poe, "I am as sick of his writings, as I am of him."

Following his sacking at the *Messenger*, Poe moved Virginia and Maria to Philadelphia and began his editorial work at *Burton's Gentleman Magazine* and *Alexander's* and then at the revamped *Graham's Lady's and Gentleman's Magazine*. At *Graham's*, Poe returned to his passion for puzzle-solving that had proven so popular at *Alexander's* and subsequently created some of the most successful and widely read work of his journalistic career. Poe once again invited his readers to submit cryptograms to challenge his skills, and he even created and published his own cryptogram, offering a year's subscription to *Graham's* to anyone who could solve it. But when *Graham's* office became inundated with answers, an overwhelmed Poe closed the contest and withdrew the offer.

During his time at *Graham's*, Poe first transmuted his journalistic passions for the analytical nature and logical reasoning of cryptography to his prose, in what he would come to refer to as his "tales of ratiocination." "The Murders in the Rue Morgue," "The Mystery of Marie Roget" and "The Purloined Letter" introduced readers to armchair detective C. Auguste Dupin, whose use of his powers of deduction and analysis to solve confounding mysteries that befuddled the inept police captivated readers. Today, this recipe for a detective story seems obvious and can be found in countless television shows, movies and paperbacks, but for readers in the mid-nineteenth century, Poe's "tales of ratiocination" contained completely new concepts and themes, and these stories effectively created the detective story genre. Arthur Conan Doyle, who would create the Sherlock Holmes character nearly fifty years later, borrowed Poe's "ratiocination," calling it "observation and deduction" and acknowledging Poe's influence on the genre, wrote, "Where was the detective story until Poe breathed the breath of life into it?"

In the spring of 1843, Poe sold another of his "ratiocination" stories, titled "The Gold-Bug," to *Graham's* for $52, but when Poe learned that

Philadelphia's *Dollar Newspaper* was sponsoring a contest for best short story with a grand prize of $100, he asked *Graham's* to return it. "The Gold-Bug" won the contest and was subsequently published in two installments in the *Dollar Newspaper* on June 21 and 28 and printed concurrently in three installments in Philadelphia's *Saturday Courier* on June 24, July 1 and July 8. The public's response to "The Gold-Bug" was enthusiastically positive, with one reviewer declaring the story "the most remarkable work of fiction published in the last fifteen years." It proved so popular that the publishers of the *Dollar Newspaper* were forced to print extra copies to meet reader demand and even took out a copyright on the story to protect their surprising windfall. Poe estimated that less than one year after first being published, more than three hundred thousand copies of "The Gold-Bug" had been circulated.

An original illustration by F.O.C. Darley that accompanied "The Gold-Bug" when Poe's story was published in Philadelphia's *Saturday Courier* in 1843. Darley had signed a contract earlier that year to illustrate Poe's ultimately unrealized periodical *Stylus*.

"The Gold-Bug" was unlike any story Poe had written before or would write again—not just in its popularity and financial success but also in the context of the story itself. J.W. Ocker, author of *Poe-Land*, gives my favorite description of the uniqueness of "The Gold-Bug": "It's a strange one for a Poe story. Nobody dies. The appearance of madness is actually cleverness. And everybody gets rich and lives happily ever after. The only real Poesque trait to the story is the deciphering of the map, which plays into Poe's love of cryptograms, and which is similar to his stories of ratiocination."

While told by a first-person narrator, like most of Poe's tales, "The Gold-Bug" bears its greatest distinction in Poe's abandonment of another of his prose hallmarks—the Gothic-influenced leitmotif of setting the story in a nondescript, mysterious location. "The Gold-Bug" is set in a specific location that is crucial to the story. It begins, "Many years ago, I contracted an intimacy with a Mr. William Legrand. He was of an ancient Huguenot family...he left New Orleans, the city of his forefathers, and took up residence at Sullivan's Island, near Charleston, South Carolina. This Island is a very singular one. It consists of little else than the sea sand, and is about three miles long."

Essentially a tale of the hunt for pirate treasure, "The Gold-Bug" weaves Lowcountry landscape, history, legend and lore around the discovery and deciphering of one of Poe's beloved cryptograms. The tale begins on "a day of remarkable chilliness" in October as the story's narrator visits his friend William Legrand and a freed slave named Jupiter, with whom Legrand shares a small hut "not far from the eastern or more remote end of the island." This side of the island clearly made an impression on Poe while stationed at Fort Moultrie, and his recollections of the more mysterious side of the island are authentic.

In an interview for the foreword of a 1969 republication, acclaimed Charleston artist Elizabeth O'Neill Verner, whose family spent every summer on the island in the late nineteenth century, recalls the eastern end of the island as "infinitely romantic—there were strange huts there and tramps, and no one walked that far, except, of course, he was very brave."

At his hut, Legrand is very excited to share the news of a gold-colored bug, a *Scarabaeus*, that he has found on the island that "he believed to be totally new" and wants the narrator's opinion on his discovery. Unfortunately, Legrand lent the bug to a lieutenant at Fort Moultrie, so he determines to draw a picture of his newly discovered bug for the narrator. Unable to find a piece of paper in his hut, Legrand "drew from his waistcoat pocket a scrap" that he had found on the beach that day near an old wreck of "the hull of what appeared to have been a ship's long boat." The narrator, sitting close to the hut's fireplace to warm himself against the chill, examines Legrand's drawing and exclaims to a confused Legrand, "This is a strange scarabaeus, I must confess; new to me; never saw anything like it before—unless it was a skull, or a death's-head, which it more nearly resembles than anything else that has come under my observation."

The bug, or *Scarabaeus*, described in the tale by Legrand as having "antennae" and "a brilliant gold color—about the size of a large hickory-nut—with two jet black spots near one extremity of the back, and another, somewhat longer, at the other," was long considered to be a species completely created in Poe's imagination. However, in 1910, a professor from my own alma mater of Virginia Tech, Ellison A. Smyth Jr., published a paper titled "Poe's Gold Bug from the Standpoint of an Entomologist" after making a bug-collecting visit to Sullivan's Island and Long Island (today known as Isle of Palms) and discovering a beetle previously unknown to the professor. In his paper, Professor Smyth explains that he believes that Poe's gold bug is a composite of the characteristics of two different beetles that can be found in the Lowcountry, including his newly discovered beetle, of which Professor Smyth writes, "The insect was new to me....It gleamed with shining fiery gold, soft satiny green, and dull old gold, and such antennae!"

Measuring about one and a half inches long and boasting powerful pinching jaws, the "shining fiery gold" beetle that Smyth encountered was the *Callichroma splendidum*. And while the species does match Poe's bug in some ways, particularly in its golden luster, it does not possess the two "jet black spots" as described by Legrand. Smyth points to another insect more easily and frequently found in the Lowcountry, the *Alaus oculatus*, commonly referred to as the "click beetle" or "jumping Jack" and its large, rounded, black eyelike spots, edged with white on its thorax, as the second half of the inspiration for Poe's gold bug.

Known as the *McKee Daguerreotype*, this likeness of Poe was taken around 1842. Bearing little resemblance to later, more celebrated images of Poe with his signature mustache, which he did not wear until the last years of his life, the *McKee Daguerreotype* photograph shows Poe as he would have appeared around the time of his writing of "The Gold-Bug."

But while the gold bug, whether born of inspiration or invention, impels the action of the tale, Poe knew that the reader's main interest lay in solving the story's cryptogram. Legrand discovers that the cryptogram has been written in invisible ink on the same scrap of paper upon which he had drawn his picture for the narrator. The cryptogram is only revealed when the parchment is "subjected to the action of fire." This exposure to the heat of a fire also reveals the image of the narrator's previously described "death's-head," and then, as Legrand explains, "Diagonally opposite to the spot in which the death's-head was delineated, the figure of what I at first supposed to be a goat. A closer scrutiny, however, satisfied me that it was intended for a kid." Legrand connects the image of the "kid" and the fact that the paper was found near the wreck of an old longboat with the infamous pirate Captain Kidd and comments, "Well; you have heard, of course…the thousand vague rumors afloat about money buried, somewhere upon the Atlantic coast, by Kidd and his associates."

The red-tinted cryptogram that emerges between the "death's-head" and the "kid" reads:

53‡‡†305))6;4826)4‡.)4‡);806*;48†8¶60))*
*85;1‡(::‡*8†83(88)5*†;46(;88*96*?;8)*‡(;48*
5);5†2:*‡(;4956*2(5*—4)8¶8*;4069285);)6†*
*8)4‡‡;1(‡9;48081;8:8‡1;48†85;4)485†528806**
81(‡9;48;(88;4(‡?34;48)4‡;161;:188;‡?;

Poe, perhaps deciding to limit the strain on the casual reader, inserted a fairly simple form of cipher in "The Gold-Bug," with each letter always represented by the same symbol or character. Even Legrand comments on the pirate's cryptogram, stating, "The solution is by no means so difficult as you might be led to imagine from the first hasty inspection of the characters" and unriddles the cryptogram as "a good glass in the Bishop's hostel in the Devil's seat—forty-one degrees and thirteen minutes—northeast and by north—main branch seventh limb east side—shoot from the left eye of the death's head—a bee-line from the tree through the shot fifty feet out."

Poe has Legrand, Jupiter and the narrator strike westward into the mainland, following the cryptogram's clues to search for the pirate treasure, and here, Poe takes his first creative liberties with his former Lowcountry home, adding "cliffs and rocks" to the area's pan-flat landscape and inventing a rocky "Devil's seat" in a cliffside, from which Legrand, with a "good glass," is able to see a skull nailed high in a tulip tree.

In his 1941 *Edgar Allan Poe: A Critical Biography*, Arthur Hobson Quinn does give a possible, though in my opinion unlikely, local substantiation of Poe's "cliffs and rocks," adding the details of an interview with Laura Bragg, a former director of the Charleston Museum. Quinn explains, "Miss Laura Bragg…has called my attention to a lime kiln on the eastern side of the Isle of Palms, which might have suggested to Poe the 'rocky seat.'"

Jupiter climbs high into the huge tulip tree, and after some confusion in discerning his left from his right side, he correctly drops the gold bug, which Legrand has attached to a string, through the skull's left eye to mark a spot to dig. After an hour and a half, Legrand, Jupiter and the narrator uncover "a mass of human bones, forming two complete skeletons" resting on top of "an oblong chest of wood…three feet and a half long, three feet broad, and two and a half feet deep." After hauling the treasure back to Legrand's hut and taking inventory of the chest's contents, the men estimate the treasure's value "at a million and a half dollars."

Poe takes another creative leap in "The Gold-Bug" in his interpretation of Charleston pirate history and the linking of the story's treasure with Captain Kidd. There is no record of Captain Kidd visiting the South Carolina coast, much less burying a treasure there. Poe likely chose Kidd because he is famously one of the few pirates who legend and historical records actually agree did bury his treasure. Kidd himself even tried to use his buried treasure as a bargaining chip to avoid the noose, offering tantalizing clues from his jail cell in London until his time ran out in May 1701. Professional and amateur treasure hunters alike have been searching for Kidd's treasure for more than three centuries.

But while Kidd may not have been part of Charleston's piratical past, I can personally attest to the fact that Poe had no shortage of Charleston pirate history to draw on for inspiration when penning "The Gold-Bug." Blackbeard, Stede Bonnet, Richard Worley, Anne Bonny and "Calico" Jack Rackham all made their mark on Charleston's pirate history, but it is a lesser-known, yet still accessible to Poe, pirate story of the Spanish brigantine the *Cid Campeador* that seems the likely candidate for the inspiration for "The Gold-Bug."

Found within a collection of affidavits held by a Charleston judge probate named Patrick E. Gleason, there are records from 1745 regarding a Spanish captain named Julian de Vega, master of the *Cid Campeador*, who had forged an alliance while in St. Augustine with an unnamed pirate to steal the *Cid Campeador*'s cargo of "silver and gold, the sum therof in English sterling being £5,800,000" and bury it on Isle of Palms. The Spanish brig rendezvoused with the pirate schooner off Charleston in August 1745, where the treasure was "conveyed in eight small boats loaded with the coin to the shore, and it was buried."

Once on shore, it was reported, "That the mate selected a large pine tree near the shore, which was blazed with a circle with two inner cross marks on the side of the tree turned from the shore. That from this tree the mate took a bearing with a land compass—northeast 28 degrees, 15 minutes. The captain again measured a distance of about 20 chains, or nearly a quarter of a mile, the end thereof being in a marsh."

The tale takes a nefarious twist when the captain of the pirate schooner and Captain de Vega agree, "When the fleet of small boats would return from the shore the brigantine and schooner were to bear away from the fleet, the same to be lost." After the treasure was buried and the witnesses left for dead, Captain de Vega sailed north to Georgetown and intentionally wrecked the *Cid Campeador* at the entrance of Winyah Bay, intending to make the Spanish government believe the treasure had been lost. But the plan began to unravel when Captain de Vega was arrested as he was making his way back to Charleston by land to recover the treasure. And events took an even more tragic turn for the pirates as their schooner "drifted westward towards Sullivan's Island, and was cast ashore on Sand Island [Morris Island]." Those among the pirates who knew the exact location of the buried treasure were lost in the wreck. Unable to draw out of Captain de Vega the treasure's location, the affidavit of the man who had captured Captain de Vega concluded, "It would be idle to search therefor without the chart [map]….But by God's grace, this deponent desireth an order from the King's lawful officer to search therefore, and will true return make to any magistrate of the King." Perhaps the treasure of the *Cid Campeador* still lies buried and undiscovered on Isle of Palms today.

"The Gold-Bug" would make its own mark on pirate history, and more specifically pirate *legend*, contributing what would become one of the staples of any good pirate tale. The "mass of human bones, forming two complete skeletons" discovered buried on top of the story's treasure is the veritable origin of the fictional pirate creed of "dead men tell no tales."

As the story concludes, the narrator asks Legrand, "What are we to make of the skeletons found in the hole?"

Legrand replies, "There seems, however, only one plausible way of accounting for them….Kidd must have had assistance in the labor. But this labor concluded, he may have thought it expedient to remove all participants in his secret. Perhaps a couple of blows with a mattock were sufficient… perhaps it required a dozen—who shall tell?"

In an essay about the creation of *Treasure Island*, Robert Louis Stevenson, whose classic pirate tale gave us no less than Long John Silver, peg legs and "fifteen men on a dead man's chest," directly attributes Poe's influence on his story's iconic "Flint's pointer," the skeleton of a pirate whose bones literally point to a treasure: "No doubt the skeleton is conveyed from Poe….I had called the islet 'Skeleton Island,' not knowing what I meant, seeking only for the immediate picturesque, and it was to justify this name that I broke into the gallery of Mr. Poe and stole Flint's pointer."

But setting piratical influences aside, there is one more possible local inspiration for "The Gold-Bug" that is worth investigating. Although its evidence is purely circumstantial, the telling and retelling of this specific link to Poe, and its subsequent link to "The Gold-Bug," over the last century has pushed it from rumor to legend and finally to Charleston tradition. This is the connection, or *possible* connection, between Poe and Dr. Edmund Ravenel.

Born on December 8, 1797, at Wantoot Plantation in Berkeley County, Edmund Ravenel was the son of Huguenot descendants Daniel and Catherine Prioleau. In 1819, Ravenel graduated with a degree in medicine from the University of Pennsylvania and thereafter began to practice in Charleston. Active in the planning and organization of the Medical College of South

Carolina—later named the Medical University of South Carolina—Ravenel served as the chair of the chemistry and pharmacy departments for ten years. The good doctor kept a residence and office on Meeting Street, and in 1835, he purchased the Grove, a rice plantation on the Cooper River. However, during the summer months, Ravenel lived and practiced on Sullivan's Island, and this time spent on the island inspired his only medical writing of note, "The Advantages of a Sea-Shore Residence in the Treatment of Certain Diseases, and the Therapeutic Employment of Sea Water."

It was during one of those summers on Sullivan's Island, specifically in the summer of 1828, that Charleston tradition has Ravenel meeting and befriending Poe.

Dr. Edmund Ravenel. *Courtesy of the Waring Historical Library, MUSC, Charleston, SC.*

Ravenel, who would have been thirty years old—eleven years Poe's senior—allegedly formed a friendship with Poe over the most mundane of hobbies—collecting seashells. It is true that Ravenel counted conchology as one of his interests and studies. He amassed a collection of more than 3,500 shells in his lifetime, and in 1834, Ravenel discovered the Lettered Olive, which is now the South Carolina state shell. Those who give credence to a relationship between Poe and Ravenel cite Poe's own passion for conchology, as expressed in his writing of the 1839 *The Conchologist's First Book*. But describing Poe as the author of *The Conchologist's First Book* is not exactly accurate.

In 1838, English writer and lecturer Thomas Wyatt published a book on conchology to be used in schools. It featured drawings and a listing of animals and shells by French naturalist Georges Cuvier. Wyatt was facing difficulty in convincing his publisher, Harper Publishing of New York, to print subsequent editions because of the book's relatively high cost. Unwilling to settle on publishing a cheaper version, Wyatt asked Poe, who Wyatt claimed "needed money very sorely at the time," to write a preface and introduction and put his name on the title page in exchange for fifty dollars. Wyatt hoped that adding Poe's relatively famous name would not only boost sales but also convince Harper's to reprint subsequent editions of his book in its original, more expensive format.

Poe readily agreed to the fifty dollars, and, in all fairness to Poe, he did actually offer more than just his name and an obligatory preface and introduction to the book. He also translated the animals and shells listed by Cuvier from French and even reorganized the book's layout. However, the easy fifty dollars came back to haunt Poe eight years later when charges of plagiarism were lodged against him by parties unaware of his deal with Wyatt. Poe defended himself against the charges in a letter written on February 16, 1847, threatening to sue those who had accused him: "I published a book with the title—*The Conchologist's First Book*, arranged expressly for the use of schools...my name being put to the work, as best known and most likely to aid its circulation....The very title-page acknowledges that the animals are given 'according to Cuvier.' This charge is infamous, and I shall prosecute for it." In a cruel bit of irony, *The Conchologist's First Book* would be Poe's only book to go into its second edition during his lifetime.

So, perhaps Poe's shared passion for seashells with Dr. Ravenel has been exaggerated over the last century and a half. But for those who insist on a bond between Poe and Ravenel, "The Gold-Bug" offers proof-positive evidence of Dr. Ravenel's inspiration and influence in the character

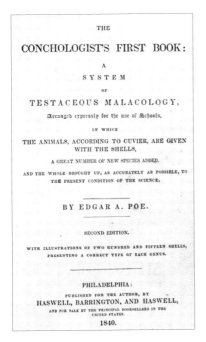

THE

CONCHOLOGIST'S FIRST BOOK:

A

SYSTEM

OF

TESTACEOUS MALACOLOGY,

Arranged expressly for the use of Schools,

IN WHICH

THE ANIMALS, ACCORDING TO CUVIER, ARE GIVEN
WITH THE SHELLS,

A GREAT NUMBER OF NEW SPECIES ADDED,

AND THE WHOLE BROUGHT UP, AS ACCURATELY AS POSSIBLE, TO
THE PRESENT CONDITION OF THE SCIENCE,

BY EDGAR A. POE.

SECOND EDITION.

WITH ILLUSTRATIONS OF TWO HUNDRED AND FIFTEEN SHELLS,
PRESENTING A CORRECT TYPE OF EACH GENUS.

PHILADELPHIA:

PUBLISHED FOR THE AUTHOR, BY
HASWELL, BARRINGTON, AND HASWELL,
AND FOR SALE BY THE PRINCIPAL BOOKSELLERS IN THE
UNITED STATES.

1840.

Title page of *The Conchologist's First Book.*

of William Legrand. Believers find evidence in just the second sentence of the story when Legrand is described as "of an ancient Huguenot family." More proof is found when Poe writes that Legrand's "chief amusements were gunning and fishing, or sauntering along the beach and through the myrtles, in quest of shells or entomological specimens." And, of course, there is the obvious connection that Legrand lives on Sullivan's Island just like Dr. Ravenel. But there are also those who see hints of Ravenel in the narrator of "The Gold-Bug." When Legrand tries to convince the reluctant narrator to accompany him and Jupiter on their expedition to find the treasure, the narrator reveals himself as a doctor, saying to Legrand, "And will you promise me, upon your honor, that when this freak of yours is over, and the bug business settled…you will then return home and follow my advice implicitly, as that of your physician?"

I was unable to find any hard documentation of a connection between Ravenel and Poe. The fact that Poe was serving under the alias of Edgar A. Perry in 1828 complicates the issue and means that if the two had met, Dr. Ravenel probably never would have pieced together that his young beachcombing friend had actually been Edgar Allan Poe. Consequently, he probably never would have bothered to share the details of his friendship with a young army private in 1828—if it did exist—with anyone else.

To muddy the waters a little more, I will add one more possible Charleston influence for the character of Legrand in "The Gold-Bug"—Hugh Swinton Legare. As mentioned in an earlier chapter, Legare was publishing the first issue of the South's first serious magazine, *Southern Review*, just as Poe was arriving at Fort Moultrie. And, as discussed, while Poe contributing to the *Southern Review* anonymously or under a pseudonym is just conjecture, it is possible that Poe was influenced, or at least impressed, by Legare during his thirteen-month stay on the island. A meeting or friendship between Poe and

Legare is certainly just as plausible as, and perhaps even more likely than, one between Poe and Dr. Ravenel. Legare, like Ravenel, was of Huguenot descent, and some of his family did originate from New Orleans—Poe mentions in his initial description of Legrand, "He left New Orleans, the city of his forefathers." "Legare," pronounced le-gree, also shares a similar spelling to and pronunciation of "Legrand." But if Poe did pay tribute to Legare in the creation of the character Legrand, Legare sadly would never have known. He died one day before "The Gold-Bug" was first published in the *Dollar Newspaper*.

Today, "The Gold-Bug" remains one of Poe's most widely read and popular short stories. Poe himself would probably not be too surprised by that fact, claiming after the story's initial success that he had written it "for the express purpose of running," meaning to gain popular success. And until the publication of "The Raven" two years later, "The Gold-Bug" was Poe's most successful publication. When "The Raven" garnered its own critical acclaim, Poe quipped, "The bird beat the bug."

In 1844, Poe returned to Charleston as a setting for another short story, "The Oblong Box." But for this tale, Charleston only serves as a port of departure mentioned in the story's opening paragraph: "Some years ago, I engaged passage from Charleston, S.C. to the city of New York, in the fine packet-ship *Independence*, Captain Hardy."

Published concurrently in *Godey's Lady's Book* and the *Dollar Newspaper*, both of Philadelphia, "The Oblong Box" is once again told in Poe's classic first-person narrator style. The story contains some measure of Poe's "ratiocination" in the narrator's use of clues—albeit unsuccessfully—to try to solve the mystery of the contents of an oblong box "about six feet in length by two and a half in breadth" that a fellow passenger sailing on the *Independence*, a morose young artist named Cornelius Wyatt, retains in his cabin. The narrator of the tale becomes consumed with the box's contents and eventually comes to speculate that it contains no less than a copy of Leonardo da Vinci's *The Last Supper*. He believes his suspicions confirmed when he overhears Wyatt pry open the box one night, followed by a "low sobbing, or murmuring sound." The narrator concludes, "He had opened his oblong box, in order to feast his eyes upon the pictorial treasure within." However, when the *Independence* breaks up in a storm a few days later, forcing the passenger to abandon ship, Wyatt shocks his fellow passengers when he lashes himself to the box, and "in another instant both body and box were in the sea—disappearing suddenly, at once and forever." When the narrator meets Captain Hardy by chance a month later, the captain explains that

Wyatt's box had contained his partially embalmed wife, which Wyatt was conveying to her mother in New York. The creepiness of Poe's tale comes full circle with the realization that on that night the narrator had overheard Wyatt pry open the box—now known to be a veritable coffin—he was doing so to gaze upon his dead wife.

Poe visited Charleston in one last short story, also published in 1844, that would ultimately come to be called "The Balloon Hoax." Much like "The Oblong Box," "The Balloon Hoax" has a minimal reference to Charleston, with the Lowcountry serving as a destination rather than a point of departure. "The Balloon Hoax" tells the fictional story of the first successful trans-Atlantic crossing by hot air balloon and contains characteristics of Poe's "ratiocination," but in reverse. Rather than breaking events and clues apart to solve a larger puzzle, "The Balloon Hoax" builds up fiction to make the event seem true. It also features one of Poe's often overlooked passions, of which he was an early pioneer—science fiction.

Poe sold the story to the *New York Sun* shortly after moving to New York from Philadelphia in the spring of 1844. The *Sun* editors, obviously impressed by Poe's tale, did not choose to bury the story deep in the pages of the April 13, 1844 edition but rather ran the story on the front page with a bold, twelve-point deck: "ASTOUNDING INTELLIGENCE BY PRIVATE EXPRESS FROM CHARLESTON VIA NORFOLK!—THE ATLANTIC OCEAN CROSSED IN THREE DAYS!!—ARRIVAL AT SULLIVAN'S ISLAND OF A STEERING BALLOON INVENTED BY MR. MONCK MASON!!"

On the same day, the *Sun* also printed a special edition, the *Extra Sun*, adding further details and an illustration of the balloon, the *Victoria*. The story, which the public believed to be a true news report, proved a sensation. Poe's attention to detail, particularly in the mechanics of the balloon and his naming of the character Monck Mason after real-life balloonist Thomas Monck Mason, convinced the public that the story was factual. The effect of this clever prank by the *Sun* is best told in Poe's own words in a letter to the *Columbia Spy*: "On the morning (Saturday) of its announcement, the whole square surrounding the 'Sun' building was literally besieged, blocked up.…I never witnessed more intense excitement to get possession of a newspaper. As soon as the first few copies made their way into the streets, they were bought up, at almost any price.…I tried, in vain, during the whole day, to get possession of a copy."

By the afternoon, the rival *New York Herald* was calling the *Sun*'s bluff, countering that the hoax was "blunderously got up" and "ridiculously put together" and first dubbing Poe's tale "The Balloon Hoax."

The headline and illustration of the hot air balloon, *Victoria*, that accompanied Poe's story "The Balloon Hoax" in the *New York Sun* on April 13, 1844.

The following Monday, the *Sun* ran a sober disclaimer, stating, "The mails from the South last Saturday night not having brought confirmation of the arrival of the balloon from England, we are inclined to believe the intelligence is erroneous."

"The Balloon Hoax" concludes with the balloon landing on the beach near Fort Moultrie and one last recollection by Poe of his former Sullivan's Island home:

> *The balloon was brought over the beach (the tide being out and the sand hard, smooth, and admirably adapted for a descent), and the grapnel let go, which took firm hold at once. The inhabitants of the island, and of the fort, thronged out, of course, to see the balloon....The balloon was exhausted and secured without trouble; and when the MS. from which this narrative is compiled was dispatched from Charleston, the party were still at Fort Moultrie.*

4

ANNABEL LEE AND THE MOURNER

I asked myself—"Of all melancholy topics what, according to the universal understanding of mankind, is the most melancholy?" Death was the obvious reply. "And when," I said, "is this most melancholy of topics most poetical?" From what I have already explained at some length the answer here also is obvious— "When it most closely allies itself to Beauty: the death then of a beautiful woman is unquestionably the most poetical topic in the world, and equally is it beyond doubt that the lips best suited for such topic are those of a bereaved lover."
—Edgar Allan Poe, "The Philosophy of Composition"

Sometimes history is hard to find. Sometimes it is hiding in an old newspaper preserved on a roll of blotchy microfilm. Sometimes it is concealed in the pages of a long-forgotten diary with pages that have not been turned in a century. Sometimes the specific piece of history that you are looking for is hiding in the footnotes of a book of a seemingly unrelated subject. Then, of course, once you open the door to the subject that you previously considered disparate, you lose focus and end up going off on a historical tangent. I have lost whole days in a library chasing disconnected stories down history rabbit holes. When you add generations of folklore, divergent oral histories and legends to your research, decoding history becomes even more difficult and frustrating. It is easy to find yourself lost in the weeds.

And sometimes you find that history is lost in the weeds—literally, lost in the weeds.

The plaque on the wrought-iron fence of the Unitarian Church on Archdale Street in downtown Charleston reads:

The Unitarian Churchyard
Since 1837 plants and tree have grown in a wild but cultivated fashion among the numerous tombstones in this Unitarian Churchyard. Caroline Howard Gilman (1794–1888), the wife of pastor Samuel Gilman (1791–1858), created a garden cemetery in the European and English traditions of churchyards, creating a place for quiet reflection and recreation and habitat for local plant species.
The grounds are meant to be a botanical treasure that also reflects the Unitarian mission to respect the interdependent web of all existence.

Allow me to summarize—the Unitarian Church graveyard is purposely unkempt and overgrown.

Built in the English Perpendicular Gothic Revival style, the Unitarian Church is the second-oldest church on the Charleston peninsula. In the early 1770s, the Society of Dissenters, known today as the Circular Congregational Church, was outgrowing its church located on Meeting Street, situated between Queen and Cumberland Streets, and the church that would become the Unitarian Church was built one block away on Archdale Street to accommodate the enlarged congregation. Just as construction was nearing completion, the American Revolution erupted in 1775, and the church was appropriated by the colonial militia to serve as barracks. When Charleston was occupied by the British after the siege of 1780, the church was used to quarter British soldiers. In 1787, when construction was finally finished after repairs were made to damages caused by the visiting troops, the church was officially dedicated. For the next thirty years, the Meeting Street and Archdale Street churches would operate in unison, sharing the same ministers and the same sermons on Sunday mornings. However, in 1817, minister Anthony Forster and more than half of the congregation declared themselves Unitarians and founded the Second Independent Church at the Archdale Street location. In 1839, the church was re-chartered and adopted the name of the Unitarian Church. The church's unique graveyard has been a celebrated hallmark of downtown Charleston for nearly two centuries.

When the Great Charleston Fire of 1861 swept through the city, destroying many structures, including the former partner Circular Congregational Church, the Unitarian church was spared. Caroline

The "wild but cultivated" graveyard of the Unitarian Church. *Photo by Jennifer Taylor.*

Gilman, wife of then-pastor Samuel Gilman, wrote after the fire, "There stood our Church in all its beauty and our cemetery with not a rose-bud crushed."

It is fortunate that the fire, whether steered by providence or naturally occurring winds, did not reach the graveyard surrounding the Unitarian Church. The wild, overgrown vegetation that defines the graveyard's landscape certainly would have offered ample kindling to the blaze. So dense is the sea of flora that all but the largest gravestones lie obscured. Spanish moss drips heavily from nearly every tree and forms almost a canopy over the hallowed ground. But the sign on the fence is accurate, it is "wild but cultivated." When searching in a specific area of the graveyard, like I did, there is chaos—vines and weeds twist and tangle in all directions. But when viewed broadly and collectively, there is form and function. Above all there is beauty.

The cemetery's southern boundary straddles the peaceful Gateway Walk, which was designed by the Garden Club of Charleston and opened in 1930. The brainchild of Clelia Peronneau McGowan, who was inspired after visiting a tranquil garden in the center of busy Paris, the Gateway Walk is named after the series of wrought-iron gates that stand along its course. The walk begins at the gates of St. John's Lutheran Church, next door to the Unitarian Church, and crosses King and Meeting Streets before concluding at St. Philip's Episcopal Church, offering a secluded, tranquil path through the center of the city. The section paralleling the Unitarian Church is arguably the most charming portion of the walkway and enhances the graveyard's naturally occurring beauty.

The day that I searched for a specific gravestone at the Unitarian Church, I did not enjoy the graveyard's "cultivated" or naturally occurring beauty. I waded waist-deep into the "wild" growth enveloping a family burial plot while mnemonic rhymes from my days of being a Boy Scout were running through my mind: "Red touches yellow, kills a fellow. Red touches black, friend of Jack." No, that was the one about how to differentiate between a poisonous coral snake and harmless king snake. It was the one about poison ivy that I was trying to remember: "Leaves of three, let them be." Yes, that was the one that I was looking for.

Unfortunately, it seemed that all of the weeds had three leaves. I should have brought gloves.

I was looking for the grave of Annabel Lee. Yes, I do mean the Annabel Lee from Poe's famous poem of the same name. The poem begins:

It was many and many a year ago,
In a kingdom by the sea,
That a maiden there lived whom you may know
By the name of Annabel Lee;
And this maiden she lived with no other thought
Than to love and be loved by me.

She was a child and I was a child,
In this kingdom by the sea;
But we loved with a love that was more than love—
I and my Annabel Lee

The legend that the real Annabel Lee is from the Lowcountry has floated around Charleston for decades. If you ask a local what they know about Poe's connection to Charleston, aside from a reference to Poe's Tavern and their hamburgers, the response that you will most likely receive is something akin to, "Isn't Annabel Lee supposed to be buried somewhere downtown?"

In 1969, this legend seems to have come to rest, quite literally, at the Unitarian Church graveyard. A letter printed in the Charleston *News and Courier* that winter reads:

The Past Business
To the News and Courier:
   Over the past decades we have witnessed a renewed interest and sometime commitment to the ideals and philosophy of a betrayed past....For us the past is a happy hunting ground with very few cities able to compete.... Therefore by making Charleston an historical shrine the old and rarely seen parts of the city can be publicized to advantage. For example, Edgar Allan Poe's great love, Annabel Lee certainly lived at Sullivan's Island, the "Kingdom by the Sea." If the site (of her grave) is discovered it can play a role as important as the tomb of Romeo and Juliet which attracts half a million visitors each year.
C.T. Leland

The letter was written by Caroline Leland, who was a liberal arts student at the College of Charleston. Leland was part of group of Poe enthusiasts at the college who were interested in exploring and discovering connections between Poe's writing and his experiences while stationed in Charleston. An eccentric visiting professor who taught Latin and Greek, an Austrian named Alexander Lenard, was also a Poe fan and, as described later, had "gotten up to his ears in the Poe cult." A bond formed between teacher and student, and Leland and Lenard, convinced that "Annabel Lee" contained verses that referenced and described Charleston, sought to make a concrete connection between the city and Poe's Annabel Lee.

Another Leland, Jack Leland, describes in a letter to the *Evening Post* on February 5, 1979, the events that had transpired a decade earlier between Caroline Leland and Alexander Lenard:

> *A statue to Annabel Lee?*
> *Annabel who?*
>
> *The idea had its conception back in 1969 when a romantic liberal arts student from the College of Charleston and the Austrian who translated "Winnie the Pooh" into Latin found a small tombstone in the Unitarian Church cemetery along the Gateway Garden Walk....And so the trail began until, on one crisp spring morning when the snow drops and jonquils were blooming in profusion in the cemetery, the Poe cult came upon the perfect tombstone.*
>
> *It has only the initials: "A.L.R." with no dates to prove historically embarrassing.*
>
> *Since Poe was a friend of the Ravenel family, certainly one of Charleston's "high born clan," that surname was seized upon after the Poe posse went through such also high-born septs as Rutledge, Rouppel, Rhett, River and Roper—all beginning with the letter "R."*

By coincidence, Charleston's Tradd Street Press was publishing an edition of "The Gold-Bug" in 1969 at the same time as Lenard and Leland were discovering their A.L.R. tombstone. This 1969 edition included a wonderful introduction, titled "Poe on Sullivan's Island," by University of South Carolina professor Frank Durham and illustrations by the acclaimed Charleston artist Elizabeth O'Neill Verner. But it is the postscript written by Verner's daughter, Elizabeth Verner Hamilton, that proves the most intriguing part of the book. Though quite short, this postscript has been fueling the legend of the connection between the Unitarian Church and Annabel Lee for half a century.

Just prior to publishing the 1969 edition of "The Gold-Bug," someone called Caroline Leland's letter that had appeared in the *News and Courier* to Hamilton's attention. Shortly afterward—and quite by chance—Hamilton ran into professor Lenard at the post office just before he moved to Brazil.

She asked Lenard if he had put Caroline Leland up to writing the letter printed in the *News and Courier*, to which Lenard responded, "I found a tombstone in a mossy cemetery. A wonderful trysting place for lovers. I'll draw you a map."

Hamilton added the drawing of the map to her postscript, and a legend was born.

Before I describe the details of the map and the results of my own investigation in the Unitarian Church graveyard, I should tell you the story, or rather the legend, that led Lenard and Leland to search out and perhaps find the grave of the real Annabel Lee. Different versions of this legend have been passed down through the decades—I imagine the same goes with all good legends, particularly those of the oral tradition. But while there might be varying accounts, the meat and potatoes of the main storyline of all versions is the same.

The best way to tell the story is the way that tour guides tell it on ghost-walking tours where the protagonist is described as a lowly army private stationed at Fort Moultrie named Edgar A. Perry. Hints are dropped throughout the telling of the tale as to the lead character's true identity, and suspense grows as the audience senses an impending revelation. At the very end of the story, the guide springs a plot-twisting Paul Harvey–like "The Rest of the Story" moment, revealing that Edgar A. Perry is actually Edgar Allan Poe.

It is good storytelling and always elicits at least a few *ooh*s and *ahh*s from the group. Unfortunately, I have already lost the element of surprise with you, so I will just relay the short version, with Poe as our leading man.

The story begins with the young, estranged Poe on a break from his soldiering duties and walking the beach outside Fort Moultrie. The lonely Poe runs into a fellow beachcomber, island resident Dr. Edmund Ravenel, and the pair become fast friends, bonding over their shared passion for seashells.

Ravenel is a widower, his wife having died the previous year while giving birth to their daughter, Mary Louisa. Ravenel's extended family living in Charleston often visit the good doctor on the island to help with childcare. Poe is often an invited guest at Ravenel's seaside cottage and regularly joins the doctor and his visiting family for dinners. Poe delights in sharing time with his adopted Ravenel family since his relationship with his own family—particularly John Allan—has become so strained.

Among those visitors to the doctor's home is a fourteen-year-old cousin named Anna—short for Annabel—who becomes the primary caretaker for little Mary Louisa. Anna begins spending more and more time on the island and Poe quickly takes notice of the beautiful girl. Sparks fly between the teenagers, and the pair soon find themselves falling madly in love.

Poe, still stinging from the loss of his first love, Elmira Royster, does not want to tempt fate and risk losing Anna in the same way, so he quickly proposes marriage. Anna readily accepts, but there are complications. Due to her young age, Anna needs her parents' permission to marry, which poses some real problems because Anna is already betrothed to another man—the eldest son of a wealthy Charleston family. Anna's parents would certainly never allow her to forfeit a marriage to an affluent Charleston gentleman for a poor soldier with no pedigree and few prospects. Poe and Anna decide to keep their love and their engagement a secret until the opportune moment presents itself to steal away and elope.

Unfortunately for the young lovers, their secret is discovered when family members catch the pair canoodling in the dunes by the seaside. Anna is taken back to Charleston and forbidden from visiting the island or having any future contact with Poe.

But love—particularly between two teenagers—has a powerful pull, and soon Poe secretly begins venturing into the city to visit Anna. Attempting to outwit her suspicious father, Anna chooses a familiar and intimate location for her clandestine rendezvouses with Poe—the graveyard of the Unitarian Church. Anna is a regular visitor to the graveyard and knows its seclusion and tranquility because her ancestors on her mother's side of the family are buried there.

After a few passionate weeks, the couple's secret trysts in the graveyard are inevitably discovered by Anna's snooping father. Things go from bad to worse for Poe and Anna when a white dress, meant to be worn on her wedding day to Poe, is found hidden in Anna's room. Anna's father is livid and takes drastic action, confining Anna to her house and only permitting her to venture out in the company of family chaperones. A visit by Anna's father to Poe's commanding officer at Fort Moultrie ensures that Poe will not be given any future leave to return to the city and visit Anna.

Bitter and pining for his Anna, Poe paces the beach at Sullivan's Island each day like a caged animal. After several weeks pass, Dr. Ravenel cautiously approaches Poe on the beach and tells him that Anna had taken desperately ill since Poe last saw her. The good doctor tried everything he could, even briefly bringing Anna to his cottage on the island in the hopes that the sea air would revive her, but her condition rapidly deteriorated. Anna died. Her last wish was to be buried in the graveyard of the Unitarian Church wearing that white dress intended for her wedding day. Friends and family believe that Anna died of a broken heart, and Anna's father holds Poe solely responsible for her death.

Filled with sorrow and rage, Poe disobeys orders and races to the graveyard only to find that Anna's father, in a final insult to Poe, left her grave unmarked. Her father even arranged for several false graves to be dug, so even in death, Anna would be hidden from Poe. He is not even afforded the opportunity to properly pay his last respects to his lost love.

A simple marker engraved with A.L.R was placed on Anna's grave only after Poe sailed from Charleston with his regiment. Poe, many years later, would derive art from this heartbreak and pen his famous poem "Annabel Lee" as a tribute to Anna and their star-crossed love.

It is a great story, or legend, and very thematically Poe-like with love and the death of a beautiful young woman. But is it true? When Elizabeth Verner Hamilton asked Frank Durham, who wrote the introduction to the 1969 edition of "The Gold-Bug," his thoughts on the legend, Durham replied, "Annabel Lee is moonshine."

The Unitarian Church agrees with Durham. When I reached out to the church, the reply did not mince words, with a historian at the church writing, "There is no connection between Edgar Allan Poe's story and the Unitarian Church in Charleston. This myth was evidently born in the last half of the 20th century when a mischievous reader penciled in a book a 'location' for the grave in the Unitarian Churchyard of the woman who was the inspiration for Annabel Lee….Please let this myth die."

But believers in the legend point to several lines of the poem that they consider to be evidence of Poe referencing a lost love from Charleston. Within the very opening lines of the poem, a perceived connection is made with "a kingdom by the sea," which for some can only refer to one city of the period—the aristocratic antebellum Charleston with its cotton-born wealth. Further, the first line of the second stanza, "she was a child and I was a child," with reference to a specific time in Poe's life, could aptly describe the period of teenage love between him and Anna. With a little amateur forensic science, one can perhaps diagnose and attribute Anna's sudden illness and death to malaria from the line, "That the wind came out of the cloud, chilling, / And killing my Annabel Lee." The disease, which at the time was not understood to be spread by mosquitos but rather believed to be caused by bad air, was prevalent in the Lowcountry, particularly on a barrier island like Sullivan's, and the chills are a typical symptom of the disease.

And, of course, as Jack Leland mentioned in his letter to the *Evening Post*, "So that her high-born kinsman came / And bore her away from me" can only reference the Ravenels of Charleston, who can trace their prodigious Huguenot family back to the city's beginnings. Some of the conspiracy-minded have even theorized that the Annabel Lee and Charleston connection reaches beyond "Annabel Lee" and appears in the lines of Poe's most famous poem, "The Raven," written in 1845. According to this legend, when searching for the right spectral, demonic bird to deliver the poem's message of loss and hopelessness, "Nevermore," Poe first considered a parrot but instead, upon reflecting on the misery and pain the Ravenel family caused him nearly two decades earlier in Charleston, he decided on a wordplay and chose a Raven.

I admit, it is all a bit of a stretch. But there is a part of me that really wants to believe. And the ability to believe is integral to the next part of this story, or legend, because we are going to quite literally open the gateway to the paranormal.

One of the beautiful wrought-iron gates of the Gateway Walk is located on King Street, directly across from the Charleston Library Society. And it is by passing through this gate that one can gain access to the Unitarian Church graveyard. When the Gateway Walk was dedicated in 1930, Clelia Peronneau McGowan spoke to a crowd gathered at this King Street gate and read a poem:

> *Through hand-wrought gates,*
> *alluring paths lead to pleasant places.*
> *Where ghosts of long forgotten things*
> *have left elusive traces.*

The poem resonates for those, like me, who have chased hidden, and sometimes lost, pieces of Charleston's history, particularly the "elusive traces" of Edgar Allan Poe. But the poem also hints, perhaps not purposefully, at literal spirits, or ghosts, of those long dead. And there might be one spirit lurking along the Gateway Walk that is "elusive" but certainly not "long forgotten."

Charleston is a haunted city. The gateway at King Street sits near the heart of Charleston's paranormal district. If you wait near the gateway long enough on any given night, you will most likely encounter at least one walking ghost tour with a guide frightening and delighting tourists with spooky tales.

The King Street gate, located along the tranquil and secluded Gateway Walk, offers access to the graveyard of the Unitarian Church. *Photo by Jennifer Taylor.*

Directly across the street from the King Street gate, at the Charleston Library Society, there is the ghost of a bibliophile named William Godber Hinson, who donated his vast collection and still roams the library, unable to leave his precious books. Just to the east, on Queen Street, Poogan's Porch restaurant is haunted by both a wired hair dog, for whom the restaurant is named, and by an old spinster named Zoe St. Amand who, with her sister Elizabeth, lived in the house long before its conversion into a restaurant. And just a couple of blocks west, the Old City Jail is haunted by no less than America's first female serial killer, Lavinia Fisher.

But while the ghosts of these stories are all benign and the most one might hope for is the appearance of an orb or some other anomaly in a photograph taken with a phone's camera, the spirit that is alleged to haunt the Unitarian Church graveyard has been known to have a physical effect on people.

The spirit is that of a teenage girl. She is reported to wear an antiquated white dress—possibly early nineteenth century—and can be seen walking about the gravestones. Those who have seen and pursued the ghost through the graveyard have described the girl walking behind a gravestone and seemingly disappearing. Some young male witnesses have described the girl locking eyes with them, seemingly transfixed on just the individual and unaware of anyone else in a tour group. But most alarming is the report that some visitors to the graveyard have lost consciousness, overwhelmed by the site's paranormal energy. One tour guide even supposedly quit his job because of the fright he experienced at the graveyard.

The ghost, of course, is believed by many to be Annabel Lee. Heartbroken and lost between the worlds of the living and the dead, she wanders from her grave, still wearing her white wedding dress, in search of her lost love, Edgar Allan Poe. Young men whose appearance may favor a young Poe draw her attention and she tries to lure them to follow her into the graveyard for a tryst that started nearly two centuries earlier. So strong is her energy, founded in passion but laced with heartbreak, that some, particularly women, become overwhelmed and pass out.

The details of the ghost story fit neatly with the legend of the Annabel Lee grave in the Unitarian Church graveyard. The easy conclusion, and the one that you will hear on a ghost tour, is that Annabel Lee rises from the grave that Lenard and Leland allegedly found in 1969 inscribed with A.L.R.

But what about that A.L.R grave and the corresponding map that professor Lenard drew for Elizabeth Verner Hamilton? Whether Lenard had poor penmanship, or the map was simply written in haste, I can report that it is nearly impossible to read. Hamilton herself wrote of Lenard's map, "I find his writing hard to read." What is clear on the map is a large square marked "Unitarian Church" and three connected lines marking the enclosed southern portion of the graveyard from Archdale Street to the gateway entrance on King Street. Next to a small dot near where the Gateway Walk fades into a tangle of vegetation on the western side of the graveyard, there is a note that says "grave of A.L." Another note written on the edge of the map states, "A.L.R.—Annabel Lee Requiescat."

By the time of drawing the map, Lenard seems to have abandoned the idea that Anna, or Annabel, was a Ravenel, the *R* representing instead *Requiescat*, which is a wish or prayer for the repose of the dead. Since there are no records of any Ravenels being buried at the Unitarian Church, Requiescat lends a bit more credibility to the story. However, the location marked as the A.L.R. grave does not lead to any family plot or cluster of gravestones that connect to the initials *A* or *L*. In fact, in his curt response to my inquiry about the possibility of Annabel Lee's grave being within the Unitarian Church graveyard, the church's historian pointed out that the map is clearly a misrepresentation, remarking, "The 'location' is the site of the Rose family plot."

Author, historian and tour guide Mark Jones also thinks that the map is marked incorrectly. But he believes that the grave may be found in the Lee family plot, which is located somewhat near the site marked A.L.R. but closer to the southern wall of the church. This would obviously make more sense, with Lee being Annabel's middle name. The Lee name would also add credence to the part of the legend that claims Anna's, or Annabel's, family on her mother's side were buried at the Unitarian Church. In my own search, I could not find any stone marked with A.L.R. at either the site marked on the map or in the Lee family section of the graveyard. In both locations, there are plenty of illegible and broken stones. The earthquake of 1886 caused extensive damage to many of the gravestones. One of these fractured or worn stones may in fact be the A.L.R. stone, but weather and time have erased any chance of reading their inscriptions. The heavy blanket of vegetation makes it very difficult to perform a deep, extensive or methodical search of any area of the graveyard and the labor-intensive process of clearing weeds, flowers and vines quickly gives way to a feeling of disrespect and desecration, which is what ultimately caused me to abandon my investigation. I did not get a poison ivy rash, but I also did not find Annabel Lee.

So, I do not know what Leland and Lenard did or did not find in the Unitarian Church's graveyard in 1969. Frank Durham may have been right when declaring the Annabel Lee legend to be "moonshine." It certainly could all be untrue—the star-crossed love of Poe and Anna, the A.L.R grave, Anna's ghost haunting of the graveyard. All of it. But there is one more piece to the story, or legend, of Charleston's connection to Annabel Lee.

This part of the story links a completely different Anna from Charleston's past to Edgar Allan Poe—an Anna who Poe never even knew. An Anna who died before Poe was even born. Another heartbroken man's Anna. An Anna who can probably be accurately described as the inspiration for Poe's penning of "Annabel Lee."

The poem "Annabel Lee" first appeared in the *New York Tribune* on October 9, 1849, two days after Poe's death. Rufus Wilmot Griswold, Poe's controversial literary executor, added the poem to his obituary of Poe in the *Tribune*. The poem would appear a few weeks later in the *Southern Literary Messenger*, but the first authorized publication would not come until January 1850 in *Sartain's Union Magazine*, as Poe gave a copy of the poem to the magazine's owner, John Sartain, to repay a five-dollar debt. Poe most likely wrote the poem in the spring of 1849—five months before his death. That spring, in a letter Poe wrote to Nancy Richmond, who Poe affectionately referred to as Annie, there is the first mention of the poem. Poe wrote, "I have written a ballad called 'Annabel Lee,' which I will send you soon."

The mystery of who exactly Poe had written "Annabel Lee" for and about began almost immediately after it appeared in the *Tribune*. More than a few women in Poe's life fit the profile of the poem's tragic, lost Annabel Lee, and theories ranged from Poe's birth mother to his childhood crush Jane Stanard to his foster mother Frances Allan. But most believe that it was written about Poe's wife, Virginia. Frances Osgood, one of Poe's love interests toward the end of his life, and herself a potential candidate for the inspiration for "Annabel Lee," believed Virginia Clemm to be the subject of the poem and wrote Rufus Griswold, "The exquisite pathos of the little poem lately written of which she [Virginia] was the subject, and which is by far the most natural, simple, tender and touchingly beautiful of all his songs."

"Annabel Lee" weaves two of the classic characteristics of Poe's writing style—a Gothic setting and a Romantic theme. The mysterious and unnamed "kingdom by the sea," with its imagery of a "sepulcher there by the sea," fits the dark, foreboding Gothic mold. His fixation on the Romantic elements of the death of a beautiful, young woman and the unceasing sorrow that premature death brings dominates the verses. Many people of the Romantic period viewed young love to be the purest form, with adulthood being the corruptor of the emotion, and as Poe writes, "She was a child and I was a child." He expounds on this Romantic notion, describing a young love so strong and pure that not only adults but even the angels are jealous, "But our love it was stronger by far than the love /

Of those who were older than we— / Of many far wiser than we…. / The angels, not half so happy in Heaven went envying her and me."

The poem has a musicality to it. The heavy use of the refrains "in this kingdom by the sea" and "of the beautiful Annabel Lee" give the poem a musical rhythm. And although the poem's stanzas have a somewhat irregular length and structure, the continual repetition of the words "me," "Lee" and "sea" maintain the poem's lulling, steady pace. Whether it is Poe's talents or just my infantile enjoyment of the repetition of words with a long *E*, "Annabel Lee" has always been my favorite poem and it made a most unlikely appearance in my life shortly after I moved to Charleston, while chasing pirate history.

When I began researching for my first book about the history of piracy in Charleston, one of my first stops was at the Charleston Library Society on King Street. My discussion with the librarian working the front desk that day began with trying to identify the library's available resources on local pirate history, but our conversation rapidly lost its focus and we soon began discussing buried treasure. That, in turn, led to a discussion of "The Gold-Bug" and the story's buried treasure, which then inspired our conversation to twist to the history of Poe's time in Charleston. I was trying to redirect the conversation back to piracy when the librarian said rather matter-of-factly, "Did you know that Poe stole 'Annabel Lee' from a poem written into the *Charleston Courier* in 1807?"

That would turn out to be one of those days when I found myself down a history rabbit hole.

The librarian produced a copy of the *Journal of English and Germanic Philology* from April 1922. It contained an article written by Robert Adger Law titled "A Source for Annabel Lee." Adger shares a poem titled "The Mourner" printed in the *Charleston Courier* on December 4, 1807, with a modest introduction by the poem's author, who identifies himself only as D.M.C:

Messrs. Editors,
I will trouble you with an occasional trifle, if you can spare it a corner

The Mourner
How sweet were the joys of my former estate!
Health and happiness caroll'd with glee;
And contentment ne'er envy'd the pomp of the great
In the cot by the side of the sea.

With my Anna I past the mild summer of love
'Till death gave his cruel decree,
And bore the dear angel to regions above
From the cot by the side of the sea!

But the smile of contentment has never return'd
Since death tore my Anna from me;
And for many long years I've unceasingly mourn'd
In the cot by the side of the sea!

And her sweet recollection shall live in the mind
Till from anguish this bosom is free,
And seeks the repose which it never can find
In the cot by the side of the sea!
D.M.C.

Even the most novice appreciator of poetry, such as myself, cannot help but be struck by "The Mourner" poem's similarity to Poe's "Annabel Lee." Adger, who is clearly not a novice appreciator of poetry, better describes the two poems' similarities:

> *Every reader will note the situation and theme of both poems: a solitary mourner lamenting his separation from the long lost wife of his youth; the similarity between the names of "my Anna" and "my Annabel Lee"; the underlying cadences of both lyrics—a line of anapestic tetrameter, followed by a line of anapestic trimeter, with alternate lines rhyming; the closeness of the two refrains: "In a cot by the side of the sea," and "In a kingdom by the sea"; and of the respective conclusion: "In a cot by the side of the sea," and "In her tomb by the side of the sea." On this evidence the case must rest, but in passing one may remark on the ideas common to both poems of angels and heavenly regions, of envy, and of the dead body born away. Such coincidences and so many are, to my mind, not to be explained by the law of chances.*

I agree with Adger. I do not think it is coincidental. I believe Poe *borrowed* from "The Mourner."

Poe was accused of plagiarism more than a few times during his career. One critic, writing under the pseudonym of Outis ("Nobody"), pointed to fifteen distinct "identities," or similarities, between "The Raven" and an

The Courier.

THE WREATH OR THE ROD.

FOR THE COURIER

MESSRS EDITORS;

I will trouble you with an occasional trifle, if you can spare it a corner.

THE MOURNER.

HOW sweet were the joys of my former estate!
Health and happiness caroll'd with glee ;
And contentment ne'er envy'd the pomp of the great
In the cot by the side of the sea.

With my Anna I past the mild summer of love
'Till death gave his cruel decree,
And bore the dear angel to regions above
From the cot by the side of the sea !

But the smile of contentment has never return'd
Since death tore my Anna from me ;
And for many long years I've unceasingly mourn'd
In the cot by the side of the sea.

And her sweet recollection shall live in the mind
'Till from anguish this bosom is free,
And seeks that repose which it never can find
In the cot by the side of the sea !

D. M. C.

"The Mourner" as it appeared in the *Charleston Courier* on December 4, 1807.

97

anonymous poem called "The Bird of the Dream." Poe was also accused of plagiarizing a story titled "The Robber's Tower," which appeared in a December 1828 issue of the British *Blackwood's Magazine*, for the creation of "The Fall of the House of Usher." Even "The Gold-Bug" caused charges of plagiarism to be leveled against Poe. Newspaper editor John du Solle suggested—though quickly retracted—that Poe had stolen the idea for "The Gold-Bug" from the 1839 story "Imogine; or the Pirate's Treasure," which had been written by a thirteen-year-old schoolgirl named George Ann Humphreys Sherburne.

But the line between plagiarism and inspiration can be a slippery slope. Are the similarities between "Annabel Lee" and "The Mourner" an occurrence of plagiarism or just a case of inspiration? And how and why would Poe have read and then copied a poem printed in a Charleston newspaper more than two years before he was born?

It is plausible that Poe took notice of "The Mourner" when the poem was picked up and printed by other newspapers well after its initial Charleston publication in perhaps a Baltimore or Richmond newspaper. But more likely, Poe discovered the poem while stationed in Charleston during his army service. An advertisement on the page following "The Mourner" gives a clue as to why Poe may have taken notice of the poem. It is an advertisement for a play titled "The Grandfather's Will" to be performed that night at the Charleston Theatre. The play was to be performed by Alexandre Placide's company.

Could a teenage Poe, serving in the army at Fort Moultrie under a false name, alone and estranged from his foster family in Richmond, have been seeking a connection to his past by poring over old Charleston newspapers for playbills and reviews of stage performances for Placide's company, of which both of his parents were once members? Did he follow the drama of that 1797–98 winter season, like I did, and read Sollee's scathing letters about Poe's namesake, Hayden Edgar, and the threats of arresting his mother's stepfather for her stolen dress? Did he find those critical reviews of his father's debut season in winter 1804 that mocked his stage fright? And did he find the playbill of his mother's return to the Charleston stage in January 1811, when Poe was just turning two years old? I believe Poe did. I believe that in his search to find a connection to his parents, he stumbled across D.M.C.'s "The Mourner" and jotted it down on a scrap of paper or tucked it away in a corner of his mind until he composed "Annabel Lee" more than twenty years later.

I wanted to discover the identity of D.M.C., first because I felt that after more than two centuries, this mysterious author deserved some recognition for inspiring one of the most famous poems in American literature. And second, because I genuinely felt bad for D.M.C. His poem is so heartbreakingly melancholic. The verses seethe with despair and desolation. "And for many long years I've unceasingly mourn'd" is, for me, the most poignant and profound and evokes a true sense of empathy for the tortured poet.

But it turned out that those feelings of compassion and heartbreak I felt for D.M.C. were short lived. I found another poem from D.M.C. printed in the *Courier* a little more than a month later, on January 19, 1808, that seemed to prove that Anna was, in fact, very much alive. In this poem, D.M.C. decries his love for Anna but warns that he will not wait around forever for her to reciprocate.

> ANNA, *do you really love me,*
> *Or by playing pert coquette,*
> *Do you only wish to prove me?*
> *Know then I'm your lover yet.*
>
> *Let then, if you wish to marry,*
> *Reason's gentle power persuade,*
> *Lest all your blandishments miscarry*
> *And you be doom'd to die a maid!*

In a poem printed on May 31, it appears that Anna decided not to "be doom'd to die a maid!" and agreed to marry D.M.C. In this poem, D.M.C. uses a repeated refrain much like he did with "in the cot by the side of the sea":

> *Since me, my dear Anna, consented to wed,*
> *In the sweet little bow'r at the foot of the hill.*
>
> *Each day with new transport to memory's view,*
> *We bring the fond hour, when the exquisite thrill*
>
> *Of love warm'd the breast; and the promise renew,*
> *We made in the bow'r at the foot of the hill.*

D.M.C. was quite a prolific poem writer—and romancer. Many poems signed by the mysterious D.M.C. appear in the *Courier* from late 1807 through 1808, and Anna was not the only source of poetic inspiration. The day after "The Mourner" appeared, D.M.C. wrote a poem that starts with "Eliza I have asked you oft, / If ever you design'd to marry." A few weeks later, D.M.C. penned a poem titled "On a Female Gamester," in which he chastises a woman named Celia for playing cards and cussing. A poem titled "To Mira" starts, "Silly girl, ah! why deceive me, / When you vow'd a mutual flame?" In another, D.M.C. described his passions for a woman named Harriet. And in one seemingly uninspired effort, D.M.C. wrote four short verses titled "To a Lady in Charleston."

Some other aspiring poets living in Charleston in 1808 apparently were not fans of D.M.C.'s body of work. The *Courier* printed several poetic-styled critiques of D.M.C.'s work that not only disparaged his poetry but also poked fun at his mysterious initialed name. One amateur bard naming himself A.B.C. (not D.M.C) started a war of rhymes with D.M.C. that escalated into a full-blown nineteenth-century poetry slam. In one particularly snarky response titled "To A.B.C.," D.M.C. wrote:

> POOR *poetasters, simple asses!*
> *You strive to scramble up Parnassus,*
> *And after thumping your dull brains,*
> *Are tumbled backward for your pains.*

I searched the Charleston City Directory for the year 1807 for individuals listed with D.M.C. as initials. I feel certain that D.M.C. lived in the city—the downtown peninsula area. His sheer number of submitted poems and quick responses to critics make it unlikely that he was living too far from where the *Courier* was printed in the city. The directory does not indicate middle names, so my search was limited to first names starting with *D* with last names starting with *C*, and I found six matching names, which included two butchers, a lumber merchant, a tanner, a watchmaker and a dry goods store manager. The poems sent by D.M.C. seem to stop near the end of 1808, so I looked for the six matching names in the 1809 directory to see if any of the names no longer appeared, theorizing that with the stoppage of his poems, D.M.C. had died or moved away. A manager of a dry goods store at 207 King Street, named Dominic Caseaux, was the only name among the six that did not appear in the 1809 directory. I tried to find more information about Caseaux by researching the history of the 207 King Street address, but I hit a dead end when I discovered that in the mid-nineteenth century, the city of Charleston renumbered street addresses on the peninsula, switching from a south-to-north numbering sequence to north-to-south. The only reference to "Caseaux" that I could find after 1808 was a listing for mail belonging to a "Madame Caseaux" to be picked up at the post office. Perhaps Madame Caseaux was the widow of Dominic Caseaux. Perhaps she was the famous Anna and the source of inspiration for "The Mourner" and consequently "Annabel Lee." Or maybe Madame Caseaux was Eliza or Celia or Mira or Harriet.

I may have failed in my efforts to identify D.M.C. or garner for him the recognition that I feel he deserves, but I hope that at least some measure of tribute will be paid to the mysterious poet by those who read this book and hopefully spare a small thought of him every time they hear or read "Annabel Lee."

5

THE SOUTH WILL WRITE AGAIN

It is evident that we are hurrying onward to some exciting knowledge—some never-to-be-imparted secret, whose attainment is destruction.
—Edgar Allan Poe, "MS. Found in a Bottle"

I have been known to give unsolicited history lectures to tourists in downtown Charleston. It is admittedly a little obnoxious, and it tends to embarrass my wife if she happens to be with me when one of my orations start, but I cannot help myself. Most often these impromptu history lessons occur when I am walking through White Point Garden and I see a group—perhaps a family—reading the pirate monument located in the northeast corner of the park. If the observers give a lingering, sincere read of the monument, and not just a passing scan, I make my move. Before the sightseers know what has hit them, they have learned more about early-eighteenth-century Charleston piracy than they certainly ever planned.

But sadly, more often than not, my lectures seem to go unappreciated and conclude not with some piratically inclined follow-up questions but with the most frequently asked question in downtown Charleston: "Do you know where there is a public restroom?" It seems everyone is looking for a restroom. Very disappointing. But I hope that at least Stede Bonnet and the dozens of other pirates hanged and buried three centuries ago at White Point Garden are grateful for my efforts to share their history.

There is another monument in White Point Garden only a hundred feet or so away from the pirate monument. And while this one is much larger and more centrally located in the park, it is woefully underappreciated by locals and tourists alike. Dedicated on June 11, 1879, the monument honors Charleston author William Gilmore Simms.

While I was still in the research phase of this book, I wanted to see if anyone visiting the park was familiar with, or maybe even a fan of, William Gilmore Simms. So, one summer evening during a bike ride, I made a stop at Simms's monument and started doing some people watching. Sitting on a bench opposite the Simms monument and not seeing much activity, it was not long before I started to get restless and had to restrain myself from engaging those who I could see nearby perusing the pirate monument. Bored and antsy from the uneventfulness, I kept reminding myself of the focus of my experiment, which was to observe people's interaction with Simms's monument—not talk pirates.

Nearly everyone who passed by did not give Simms's monument so much as a glance. A slight change in trajectory along the path to the left or right to skirt past his monument was the only indication of most people's awareness of the large stone structure. A small group that did stop at the monument to read its inscription seemed to do so more as the duty-bound action of responsible tourists and not because of any genuine, collective interest in learning about the man the monument honored. I approached this group of dutiful visitors, including one especially responsible sightseer taking pictures of the monument, and asked, "Do you know William Gilmore Simms?" The responses from the group were unanimously "no." Eyes glazed over in boredom as I listed Simms's facts, dates and writings. But then when I asked, "Do you know Edgar Allan Poe?" their eyes brightened and reengaged.

"I love Edgar Allan Poe. Did he know this guy?" asked one woman, pointing at the monument.

"Well, Poe said that William Gilmore Simms was the best writer in America," I explained, "and he said that Simms wrote the best ghost story that he ever read."

It was like magic. With the Poe connection, I could then see a renewed and sincere interest wash over the group as they gave the monument another thorough look. As I walked away, I saw smiles conjured and guts sucked in while the group positioned for a photo in front of the monument. I was pretty pleased with myself, and, perhaps most satisfying, no one asked me where they could find a public restroom.

Poe's exact words, written in 1845 while editor of New York's *Broadway Journal*, were that Simms was "immeasurably the best writer of fiction in America" and "the best novelist which this country has, upon the whole,

The William Gilmore Simms monument at White Point Garden. *Photo by Jennifer Taylor.*

produced." And Poe's comment on Simms's ghost story titled "Murder Will Out," which was the first tale in a collection called *The Wigwam and the Cabin*, was no less impressive: "We have no hesitation in calling it the best ghost story we ever read." Truly praise from Caesar.

Poe and Simms began corresponding regularly after Poe's glowing reviews appeared in the *Broadway Journal*, and Poe continued his praise of Simms in the personal letters the pair exchanged. Though Simms was probably never aware of a connection with Poe prior to their correspondences in 1845, Simms had actually encountered his new amiable pen pal nearly two decades earlier in Charleston. Poe met Simms—or at least heard Simms speak—while stationed at Fort Moultrie. A twenty-two-year-old Simms delivered an oration at Fort Moultrie on June 28, 1828, on the occasion of the fifty-second anniversary of the American victory over the British at the palmetto log fort on Sullivan's Island. Simms also published two books of Romantic verse in Charleston in 1827, *Lyrical and Other Poems* and *Early Lays*, and it is certainly possible the Romantic poetry–obsessed Poe may have read Simms's books of verse while serving at Fort Moultrie. And, while on leave from his duties, Poe may have even made a visit into the city to attend one of Simms's readings of his poetry at a local bookstore. But Poe, ever elusive about his army years, most likely never shared his past Charleston connections with Simms when the two began corresponding. There is certainly no mention of it in the letters.

William Gilmore Simms was a prolific writer during his lifetime, attempting nearly all fields of writing—poetry, fiction, drama, criticism, history, biography and journalism. Simms considered the best works of his life to be his poetry, but, much like Poe, posterity would find his fiction more enduring. Also, like Poe, Simms earned a living—or at least supplemented his income—as an editor for several different newspapers and magazines. The high tide of his editorial career came in 1845 when he took over the *Southern and Western Magazine and Review*, which was renamed *Simms's Magazine*. But while Simms and Poe shared a similar experience with their editorial ventures, their careers profoundly diverged in respect to the financial successes of their published writings. Where Poe spent most of his professional career in poverty, Simms's short novel *Martin Faber*, written in 1833, and his first major work of fiction, *Guy Rivers*, written the following year, earned him as much as $6,000 a year in royalties before he had even turned thirty years old. Simms could count himself as one of the few people living in the United States at the time who was making a living as a writer.

But while Simms certainly was one of America's most impressive writers, Poe's platitudes and puffery of him in both the *Broadway Journal* and the personal letters he exchanged with Simms were not without a not-so-hidden agenda. Poe was anxious to secure contributors for his *Broadway Journal*—specifically southern contributors. By 1845, Poe had developed a distaste for the transcendentalist literature produced in the North, particularly by Boston authors, with its philosophical sentimentality and

William Gilmore Simms.

poetry laced with moral lessons. Although Boston was the city of his birth and he had signed his first published book of poetry, *Tamerlane and Other Poems*, as "A Bostonian," Poe was condemning his hometown by 1845, writing in the November 1 edition of the *Broadway Journal*, "We like Boston. We were born there—and perhaps it is just as well not to mention that we are heartily ashamed of the fact.…Bostonians have no soul.…The Bostonians are well-bred—as very dull persons generally are." Flaunting his disdain at a sold-out lecture at Boston's Lyceum Association that same year, Poe, who was expected to recite a new poem, instead stunned and insulted the audience, delivering a lecture disparaging Boston transcendentalism and reciting the confusing and longwinded "Al Aaraaf."

With a fixed distaste for the literature produced in the North, Poe had begun to identify himself more and more as a southern writer, and he sought out other southern writers to publish and showcase his personal definition of American literature. In many of his reviews, Poe was quick—perhaps at times too quick—to celebrate southern writers and expose what he perceived to be a collective prejudice against writers born below the Mason-Dixon Line. Poe wrote of Simms that "had he been…a Yankee, [his] genius would have been rendered immediately manifest to his countrymen, but unhappily (perhaps) he was a southerner." Poe recognized not only Simms's "genius" but also his extensive relationships with many of the popular southern writers who were published in *Simms's Magazine* and other publications where he had served as editor, and he hoped that flattery could garner Simms's influence on southern contributors to add to the *Broadway Journal*.

Poe's embracing of southern literature and his abandonment of northern writers devolved by 1845 into slander, character assassinations and threatened libel lawsuits lodged by and against several minor writers from New York in what came to be called the war of the literati. Poe's reviews of these specific targeted authors from New York had gone far beyond the scope of literary criticism and into childish, personal attacks. Poe's northern targets responded in kind, with one of the writers counterattacking and, in an attempt to defame Poe, claiming that Poe had spent time in a mental asylum. Another mocked Poe's physical appearance and character: "forehead rather…low, and in that part where phrenology places conscientiousness and the group of moral sentiments it is quite flat; chin narrow and pointed, which gives his head, upon the whole, a balloonish appearance, and which may account for his supposed light-headedness."

In their letters, Poe tried to lure a reluctant Simms into being an active participant in his dirty little war, but Simms did not engage. Simms did, however, passively defend Poe by publishing consistently positive reviews of him and even defending the shape of his head in the *Southern Patriot*, writing that Poe had "a broad intelligent forehead." Simms tried to talk some sense into Poe in the wake of the war of the literati, writing him in July 1846 and encouraging him to stop wasting his time and energies on his war of words:

> *Suffer me to tell you frankly, taking the privilege of a true friend, that you are now perhaps in the most perilous period of your career—just in that position—just at that time of life—when a false step becomes a capital error—when a single leading mistake is fatal in its consequences….I need not say to you that, to a Southern man, the annoyance of being mixed up in a squabble with persons whom he does not know, and does not care to know.*

Despite his support, defense and "true friend" reference, Simms always remained wary of Poe, subtly keeping his distance from the infamous "Tomahawk Man" while remaining warm and cordial in his correspondences. Simms himself had been on the receiving end of one of Poe's virulent reviews nearly a decade earlier and well-remembered the sting.

In a letter written to James Lawson a few months before his 1846 "true friend" letter to Poe, Simms wrote, "Poe is no friend of mine, as I believe. He began by a very savage attack on one of my novels—the Partisan." This references a review Poe had written of Simms's *The Partisan*, a Revolutionary War romance, in the January 1836 edition of the *Southern Literary Messenger*.

Poe's review of *The Partisan* is written in his typical biting, aggressive style: "There is very little plot or connexion [sic] in the book before us; and Mr. Simms has evidently aimed at neither….Of the numerous personages who figure in the book, some are really excellent—some horrible….Mr. Simms' English is bad—shockingly bad….Instances of bad taste—villainously bad taste—occur frequently in the book."

The Partisan was one novel in a series of Colonial and Revolutionary War romances that proved—despite Poe's negative review—very successful for Simms. Popular for its detailed landscape descriptions and exciting battle scenes, the series built for Simms a national reputation. He followed with a less-than-successful series of romance novels set in Spain but returned to his southern roots with the well-received *Richard Hurdis* in 1838 and *Border Beagles* in 1840. The 1840s were Simms's most productive period—he published thirty-one separate titles while still finding time to edit three magazines. Among those titles was his *History of South Carolina*, which would be required reading in South Carolina schools for decades. The history concentrates largely on the Revolutionary War and expounds the themes that were implicit in all of Simms's previous Revolutionary War romances—for South Carolina the war had been a civil and internecine conflict, and as a result, the state had suffered more devastation to its property and population than the other states. In 1844, continuing his passion for the Revolutionary War, Simms published the biography *The Life of Francis Marion*—one of four biographies that he wrote between 1844 and 1849 and still considered one of the foremost researched biographies on the Swamp Fox.

Three decades before the Civil War, when South Carolina's legislature declared that the federal tariffs of 1828 and 1832 were null and void and pushed the question of states' rights to the forefront of the national consciousness in what would be called the Nullification Crisis, Simms stood firm as a unionist and opposed nullification. While editor of the *City Gazette*, Simms's editorial stance against nullification caused a political mob to gather before the newspaper's office in the fall of 1831. In 1844, Simms was elected to a two-year term in the South Carolina legislature, which he followed with an unsuccessful bid for lieutenant governor in 1846, campaigning for both under the unionist banner. However, Simms made a wholesale political shift when he married Chevillette Eliza Roach, the daughter of a prominent South Carolina planter, and inherited a large home and working plantation called Woodland, located near Orangeburg. By 1850, Simms—at that point a slaveholding, southern gentleman planter—had become a fervent secessionist and defender of states' rights. Detrimental to his career and legacy, and ultimately the reason that his monument is passed over in White Point Garden by locals and tourists alike, he had also become a zealous defender and promoter of slavery.

In 1854, as a rebuttal to abolitionist Harriet Beecher Stowe's *Uncle Tom's Cabin*, Simms published *Woodcraft*, the story of the benevolent relationship between a slave and his master in post–Revolutionary War South Carolina. It presented Simms's personal and idealized belief in the natural state of slavery. *Woodcraft* proved among the most popular of the anti-Tom or plantation genre of books, which attempted to show that either slavery was beneficial to those enslaved or the evils of slavery depicted in Stowe's book were exaggerated.

The Civil War proved devastating for Simms—he lost his only son and his home at Woodland was burned by stragglers from Sherman's army. After the war, an unrepentant Simms was unable to regain his previous acclaim and fell into financial difficulties as his books failed to find an audience. The age of realism and transcendentalism in literature that followed the Civil War was dominated by northern writers, and Simms was lumped with other southern romancers who were viewed as lacking in the qualities that formed serious literature. His ardent views on slavery, upon which he wrote extensively before and during the war, ensured that he was further marginalized, and his writings were largely purged in the postwar literary scene. A Reconstruction-era biography of Simms, written by William P. Trent in 1892, did little to resurrect interest in his works, as it presented a sympathetic but implicitly condescending depiction. Trent portrayed Simms as a victim of an antebellum southern society that stifled its writers and made it impossible for him to transcend the limitations inherent in the culture. Trent reported much of Simms's work as mediocre, not necessarily because of his lack of genius but because of the constraints of the society and the time in which he lived. Trent's characterization proved enduring, and for decades, his biography was the final word on Simms's legacy.

In the years following the war, Simms worked feverishly to support himself and several other literary friends who could not support themselves. He served as editor for three newspapers but still managed to publish three long works of fiction in the last years of his life, including his final Revolutionary War tale, *Joscelyn*. But with his market diminished, sales fell flat. The financial and personal strain proved overwhelming, and he died on June 11, 1870, from what was described as "a complete physical breakdown." Charleston fell into mourning for its native son, and as Simms's long funeral procession tracked from the city to his final resting place at Magnolia Cemetery, the bells of St. Michael's Church rang a requiem. Simms's often overlooked monument in White Point Garden, designed by sculptor John Quincy Ward and architect Edward B. White in 1878, was formally dedicated on the ninth anniversary of his death.

Another monument in downtown Charleston near the Meeting Street entrance of Washington Square Park honors one of those literary friends who Simms helped support in the years following the Civil War—poet Henry Timrod. Born in Charleston on December 8, 1828, Henry Timrod was the son of a bookbinder and amateur poet whose shop was a gathering place for Charleston's literary community. Exposure to the city's most elite writers at a young age sparked an early love of poetry in Timrod, and he began submitting poetry to the *Charleston Evening News* while still a teenager. Though he would be published in the *Southern Literary Messenger* before his twenty-first birthday and though he was considered by many to be the second-best southern poet after Poe, Timrod would be most known and recognized during his lifetime as the secessionist South's literary spokesman and eventually as the so-called poet laureate of the Confederacy.

Much like Simms, Timrod's association with the Confederacy and its lost causes of secession and slavery destined his work to go unappreciated and obscured in the postwar literary scene hegemonized by northern writers and publishers. However, Timrod's poetry did experience a revival more than 130 years after his death in the most peculiar and unlikely of forums—within the lyrics of Bob Dylan's 2006 album *Modern Times*, which would be his first album to reach number one on the U.S. charts since 1976. The conduit for Timrod's poetry appearing in Dylan's lyrics seems to be a fixation on the Civil War that Dylan has possessed for much of his life. In his memoir *Chronicles, Volume One*, Dylan recounts that in the 1960s, he systematically read every newspaper at the New York Public Library for the years 1855 to 1865. It is here that Timrod's verses most likely first entered Dylan's consciousness. Timrod biographer Walter Brian Cisco identified at least seven instances of Timrod's verse appearing in Dylan's lyrics, including, "More frailer than the flowers, these precious hours," from "When the Deal Goes Down." Compare that to Timrod's "Rhapsody of a Southern Winter Night" verses, "A round of precious hours / Oh! Her, where in that summer noon I basked / And strove, with logic frailer than the flowers."

Timrod's arrival on the pop culture scene in 2006 did cause some Poe-related confusion, with cases of mistaken identity for many who searched for more information on Charleston's poet laureate of the Confederacy, as Timrod's mustached visage bears a striking resemblance to Poe. Timrod's portrait, which hangs at the state capitol in Columbia, is often confused as a likeness of Poe. But Poe and Timrod's similarities extend beyond the physical to a common shared passion: Romantic-style poetry. Timrod's early poetry parallels much of Poe's, both stylistically and thematically, but when South Carolina set itself on a war footing, Timrod began to shape his Romantic-style verses around rallying support for the Confederacy and, as the war dragged on, memorializing its dead. While Timrod considered himself heavily influenced by Poe, he did differ from Poe in the structure and composition of poetry. In "A Theory of Poetry,"

Henry Timrod.

a lecture that Timrod gave in 1863 and was later published, he disagrees with some of the cardinal rules of poetry that Poe put down in "The Poetic Principle," such as the importance of brevity and the requirement for a poem to be short enough to read in its entirety in one sitting. Timrod challenged Poe's notion that the epic poem is a contradiction in terms. He also stood at odds with Poe's rule that poetry should be limited in subject to his so-called "sense of the beautiful." While including beauty as a source, Timrod believed that poetry must also be rooted in truth and embody moral and philosophical lessons—a principle not far removed from Poe's hated transcendentalist literature.

Timrod suffered from health issues his entire life, which prevented him from serving in his beloved Confederacy. Following the war, his maladies included tuberculosis and he was struggling to support his family. Though his most popular poem, "Ode Sung on the Occasion of Decorating the Graves of the Confederate Dead, at Magnolia Cemetery," was published shortly after the war, he was compelled to sell family silver and furniture and reluctantly accept money from friends like William Gilmore Simms to feed his family.

When Timrod died on October 7, 1867, exactly eighteen years after Poe, the details of his death seem ripped directly from the pages of one of Poe's macabre pieces of fiction. While writing in his journal on the night of October 7, Timrod suffered a massive tuberculosis-induced hemorrhage. Coughing blood onto his journal, he died at his desk with pen in hand. His final journal, saved for posterity at the Charleston Library Society, still carries the bloodstain from that fatal night and is known as the "blood book."

The views of Poe's contemporaries, like Simms and Timrod, on states' rights, secession and slavery bring natural speculation as to Poe's feelings and attitudes toward those same issues and institutions. Was Poe a racist? Had he lived another twelve years, where would his allegiances have lied when Fort Sumter was shelled on April 12, 1861?

Clues might be found in another Charleston connection, specifically in Poe's relationship with Colonel William Drayton—a member of one of Charleston's most prestigious families. Exactly when and where Poe and Drayton first met is uncertain. In a 1940 letter to Poe biographer Arthur Hobson Quinn, Dr. William Drayton Jr. wrote that Drayton family tradition holds that Poe formed a "warm" friendship with the colonel while stationed at Fort Moultrie. However, considering the fallacious nature of Poe's stint in the army—serving under a false name—it seems more likely that Poe first made Drayton's acquaintance a decade later while both were living in Philadelphia. Though the exact timeline of Poe and Drayton's meeting is disputed, what is certain is that whenever they did meet, Drayton made a strong impression on Poe, as he dedicated his 1840 collection of short stories, *Tales of the Grotesque and Arabesque*, to Drayton.

William Drayton was born in 1776 in St. Augustine, Florida, where his father served as chief justice for the Province of East Florida. In 1780, the family moved to the Drayton ancestral land in Charleston, and shortly

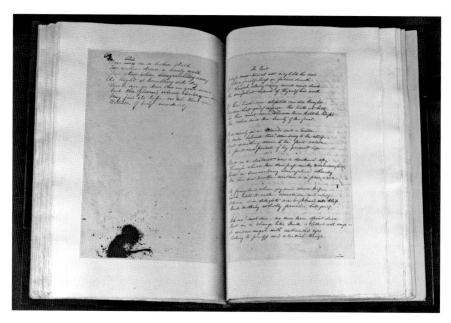

Known as the blood book, this journal is stained with the blood of Charleston poet Henry Timrod, who died during a tuberculosis-induced hemorrhage while writing on October 7, 1867. *Courtesy of the Charleston Library Society, Charleston, SC.*

thereafter, young William was sent to England to receive his education. Upon the completion of his primary education abroad, William returned to South Carolina and studied law. During the War of 1812, Drayton was commissioned as a colonel—a rank and title that he would use for the rest of his life. Following the war, Drayton entered politics, and starting in 1825, he served two terms as South Carolina's first district delegate to the U.S. House of Representatives. However, in 1833, on the heels of the Nullification Crisis, Drayton—a staunch unionist—departed Charleston and moved his family to Philadelphia, where he would live for the rest of his life.

Much like William Gilmore Simms, Colonel William Drayton, while a unionist, was an ardent and vocal supporter of slavery. In 1836, Drayton penned and published the proslavery tract *The South Vindicated from the Treason and Fanaticism of the Northern Abolitionists.* That same year, an unsigned but supportive review of Drayton's title, as well as another proslavery book by James Kirke Paulding called *Slavery in the United States*, appeared in the April 1836 edition of the *Southern Literary Messenger.* This unsigned review has been ascribed—not without debate—to Poe. And for many, the review represents the definitive conclusion to the argument on Poe's feelings toward the institution of slavery. The anonymous author of the review wrote, "Nothing is wanting but manly discussion to convince our own people at least, that in continuing to command the services of their slaves, they violate no law divine or human…society in the South will derive much more of good than of evil from this much abused and partially-considered institution."

Poe certainly possessed an empirical knowledge of slavery. There were slaves in John Allan's household, particularly after the death of Allan's uncle William Galt. An account of John Allan's business interests, quoted by Poe biographer Jeffrey Meyers, notes that Allan and his partner, Charles Ellis, "as a side issue were not above trading…old slaves whom they hired out as the coal pits till they died." Growing up in Richmond, Poe would have witnessed the full measure and harsh realities of slavery, including the frequent slave auctions held in the city. And while Poe's personal feelings toward the institution of slavery are unclear, the easiest conclusion is that Poe most likely carried the typical attitude of white superiority in the antebellum South, and he likely considered the subjugation of black people as part and parcel of southern life.

I wanted to learn more about Poe's views on race, and generally just more about Poe, so while on a trip to visit family in Virginia, I made a stop at the Poe Museum in Poe's hometown of Richmond. The museum, which started as the Edgar Allan Poe Shrine in 1922, is uniquely situated just a short distance from the city's Monument Avenue, where traffic circles loop around the famous—and some would consider *infamous*—monuments of Confederate leaders like Robert E. Lee and "Stonewall" Jackson. The museum's manager and curator, Chris Semtner, offered me a personal tour, and though I had visited the museum several times before, I was still surprised by the incredible collection of Poe artifacts. The museum, which welcomes about thirty thousand visitors per year, boasts a huge inventory of items, including Poe's cane and trunk from his mysterious final days, a pair of original life portraits of John and Frances Allan and even Poe's boyhood bed. There are original Poe writings, like the only known manuscript in Poe's handwriting of his original "To Helen" and his 1831 volume *Poems by Edgar A. Poe*, which he put together with funds collected from his fellow West Point cadets.

My tour guide, Chris Semtner, is no less impressive, seemingly channeling Poe while giving a tour and seamlessly weaving quotes and passages into even the idlest conversation. Recognizing that I was in the presence of someone who has probably forgotten more about Poe than I will ever learn in my lifetime, I feigned a deepness of intellect and framed my inquiries about

Poe's views on race by referencing the juxtaposition of the Poe Museum and the Confederate monuments a few blocks away. Clearly having considered the issue before, his response was exhaustive and surprising, even managing to tailor a connection between "The Gold-Bug" and Poe's views on race. While Semtner agreed that Poe probably shared the views on race common to most southerners of the time, he also saw examples of Poe empowering black characters in several of his stories, including "The Gold-Bug."

Contrary to many scholars' use of the work as an example of Poe's racism, with its negative characterization of Jupiter as superstitious and ignorant, Semtner points out that Jupiter, who had been manumitted, chose to stay with his former master "with a view to the supervision and guardianship of the wanderer." And though Jupiter refers to Legrand as "Massa Will," he does not hesitate to stand up to Legrand to protest, and even punish, his bad behavior. When Legrand disappears unexpectedly for an entire day, Jupiter becomes angry and explains to the story's narrator, "I had a big stick ready cut for to gib him deuced good beating when he did come." And perhaps it is not too big of a leap to speculate that some scholars' perception of Jupiter's ignorance shown in his inability to differentiate his left eye from his right was actually a savvy ruse by Jupiter, who had designs on returning to the tree to retrieve the treasure for himself.

Back in Charleston, one year after Richmond dedicated the Poe shrine that would ultimately become the Poe Museum, another monument to Poe was unveiled. Although much smaller in scale—and arguably in impression—the *Year Book of the Poetry Society of South Carolina* reported that the unveiling at the Charleston Museum in the spring of 1923 attracted a "thronging attendance, which sat on the chairs, floors, platforms, benches, overflowed from the Children's Room into the Reading Lobby; many indeed were turned away." The object of this "thronging attendance" was a small diorama consisting of a wax figure of Poe sculpted by Dwight Franklin. The wax figure stands about one foot tall and depicts Poe standing on the wind-swept beach at Sullivan's Island dressed in his military uniform and long, flowing black cape. Presented to the Charleston Museum as a gift from the ladies of the Board of the Children's Museum of Brooklyn, New York, the miniature was dedicated as Poe on Sullivan's Island, and the accompanying plaque points to the influence of the Lowcountry's landscape on Poe: "The semi-tropical scenery of the Carolina coast, its palmetto covered dunes, dark jungle pools, and deep bird-haunted swamps provided the landscape setting which Poe's imagination transmuted into the very spirit of much of his poetry and prose."

Among the speakers at the unveiling were some of the leading members of a local group called the Poetry Society of South Carolina. The elder statesman of the group was novelist, artist and poet John Bennett, a transplant from Ohio who had moved to Charleston in 1902. Most famous for his Charleston classic *Doctor to the Dead*, a collection of alternately grotesque and poignant stories collected from black storytellers in and around Charleston, Bennett was an advocate for writing in the very style and premise of Poe's "poetry and prose" described on the plaque of the diorama, the idea of drawing from local Lowcountry motifs and lore for literary art.

From this relatively simple idea, the beginnings of a Charleston literary renaissance took shape, and Bennett began hosting regular meetings of some of Charleston's most influential writers, including DuBose Heyward, best known for his novel *Porgy* and subsequent collaboration with George and Ira Gershwin on *Porgy and Bess*. At the same time that Bennett was hosting his meetings, Laura Bragg, the first female director of the Charleston Museum, was mentoring and fostering a group of local female writers that included Josephine Pinckney. The two literary groups eventually joined to create the Poetry Society of South Carolina, formed under a charter that aimed to encourage and promote all southern writers. It was a lofty and novel idea for the time, as even though it was more than half a century since the end of the Civil War, the South was still lagging far behind the North, both culturally and artistically, and northern writers still dominated the literary arts.

The burgeoning literary movement in Charleston gained a national audience and contributed to a larger movement that would come to be called the Southern Renaissance, but closer to home, the Poetry Society of South Carolina and their local- and regional-influenced writings formed one part of a boom of art, literature, architecture and historical preservation that is remembered as the Charleston Renaissance. Perhaps associated more with the visual arts than the literature produced during the period, the Charleston Renaissance showcased local artists like Elizabeth O'Neill Verner and Alice Ravenel Huger Smith, who, much like their literary cohorts, drew inspiration for their oil paintings, watercolors and prints from local architecture and landscapes. The movement also generated interest in the preservation of many of those historic homes that found their way onto Charleston Renaissance painters' canvases and sparked the creation of the Charleston Preservation Society.

Among the local motifs that the writers of the Charleston Renaissance seized upon for inspiration and content was none other than Edgar Allan Poe. Although it had been more than thirty-five years since George E.

Left: DuBose Heyward. *Right*: Hervey Allen.

Woodberry concretely linked Poe to Charleston by discovering and revealing the true identity of Private Edgar A. Perry, the members of the Poetry Society of South Carolina were the first to truly celebrate the Lowcountry's connection to Poe, with various members writing Poe into the literary tradition that they were helping to create.

In 1922, Bennett was the first of the group to write of Charleston's intimate connection to Poe when he penned an article on the subject for Columbia's *State* newspaper. That same year, DuBose Heyward and another member of the Poetry Society of South Carolina, poet and novelist Hervey Allen, guest edited an issue of *Poetry* magazine, further highlighting the Poe link. Heyward and Allen also coauthored a book of poetry called *Carolina Chansons: Legends of the Lowcountry*, and each penned a tribute to Poe for the collection.

In 1926, Hervey Allen produced the most enduring tribute to Poe of all the Charleston Renaissance writers with his enormous, two-volume Poe biography *Israfel: The Life and Times of Edgar Allan Poe*. The title references Poe's poem "Israfel," which is about an angel from the Koran, who Poe describes as "the angel Israfel, whose heart-strings are a lute, and who has the sweetest voice of all God's creatures."

Allen likens Poe to Israfel and adopts the mystic stylings of Poe's poem in his contribution to *Carolina Chansons: Legends of the Lowcountry*. His poem "Alchemy" places the narrator on Sullivan's Island, dreaming of Poe's return, summoned and conjured by the chimes of bells drifting across Charleston Harbor:

> *I think some dusk their metal voices*
> *Yet will call him back*
> *To walk upon this magic beach again,*
> *While Grief holds carnival upon the harbor bar.*
> *Heralded by ravens from another air,*
> *The master will pass, pacing here,*
> *Wrapped in a cape dark as the unborn moon.*
> *There will be lightning underneath a star;*
> *And he will speak to me*
> *Of archipelagoes forgot,*
> *Atolls in sailless seas, where dreams have married thought.*

DuBose Heyward's poem "Edgar Allan Poe" follows a more perspicuous and rhythmic pattern than "Alchemy" but once again places the narrator with Poe on Sullivan's Island. Poe is imagined as an army private and he and the narrator are on the beach, passing the predawn hours in quiet contemplation until the bugle calls a brooding Poe back to his duties at the fort:

> *Once in the starlight*
> *When the tides were low,*
> *And the surf fell sobbing*
> *To the undertow,*
> *I trod the windless dunes*
> *Alone with Edgar Poe....*
>
> *When the bugle's silver*
> *Spiralled* [sic] *up the dawn,*
> *Dew-clear, night-cool,*
> *And the stars were gone,*
> *I arose exultant,*
> *Like a man new born.*
>
> *But my friend and master,*
> *Heavy-limbed and spent,*
> *Turned, as one must turn at last*
> *From the sacrament;*
> *And his eyes were deep with God's*
> *Burning discontent.*

The most ambitious of the Poe-inspired poetic tributes from the Charleston Renaissance writers comes from Beatrice Witte Ravenel and was first published in her 1926 collection of poetry *The Arrow of Lightning*. The two-hundred-line blank verse poem "Poe's Mother" imagines and interprets the period of Poe's first visit to Charleston as a two-year-old. The poem is delivered from the perspective of Poe's mother as she sits with Eddie in the quiet early hours of a Charleston spring morning and reflects on her career, the end of her marriage, her failing health and her fears for the future of her young son:

Beatrice Witte Ravenel.

> *I love such crazy fancies, early mornings,*
> *When nothing's very real. The babies sleeping*
> *Safe islanded in small worlds of their own....*
> *The sea-breeze, slitting through the broken shutter,*
> *Magnolias, too far off to sicken one,*
> *Across the balcony where, strung with vines,*
> *The metal twists a lyre! Eddie saw it—*
> *That child sees everything. This the hour*
> *I love, the unrealest hour of all the day....*
> *And even David—O God, where is he now?—*
> *Forsake me like a tide that's going out.*
> *My cough itself grows better in this air;*
> *Mild, vivid Charleston April, lax and salty....*
>
> *What will become of him? I know, I know*
> *The child's alone!...*
> *Don't cry, my little, little, darling lamb!*
> *His mother'll wrap him in the counterpane,*
> *The pretty white-and-purple patchwork thing,*
> *And rock him on the balcony. She'll sing*
> *Of cities in the water, just like this.*

6

CHASING POE'S GHOST

...no! even in the grave all is not lost.
—Edgar Allan Poe, "The Pit and the Pendulum"

One late summer evening, I rode my bike to Poe's Tavern on Sullivan's Island to meet my wife for dinner. Wanting to keep an eye on my bike propped up against a "No Parking" sign along the sidewalk, I chose to sit at one of the outdoor bistro tables situated against the restaurant's white-picket fence. It was a busy night and most of the outdoor tables were full, as patrons were taking advantage of the sea breeze that was still blowing and not only keeping the temperature comfortable but also throwing the blood-thirsty mosquitos off the scent of the patio's warm bodies.

I was waiting for my wife to arrive and unintentionally eavesdropping on conversations around me when my attention was drawn to a group behind me walking down the restaurant's front steps. There were three people in the group and based on their accents, it was clear that none were native to South Carolina. But a quick read of the group seemed to demonstrate that they were not all tourists either. From what I could discern of the little bit of conversation that I overheard, one member of the group had recently moved to the Charleston area and was showing off his new local knowledge to two visiting friends. These two friends appeared a little worn and weary from what, I was able to decipher, had been a full day with their would-be tour guide. Dinner at Poe's Tavern was apparently just one stop on a grand tour of Charleston cuisine and culture.

Poe's Tavern on Sullivan's Island. *Photo by Jennifer Taylor.*

As the group descended the bottom step, this new Charleston local stopped and pointed to the gold bug mosaic created by local artist Sonya Sterling that is set in the cement at the bottom of the steps. He exclaimed, "This is a palmetto bug." My ears instantly perked up because I knew that whatever was coming next was going to be good stuff. I shifted in my chair and tuned in to listen to what I can only describe as an *alternative* version of the history of Edgar Allan Poe and "The Gold-Bug."

In this divergent version, it seems that Poe was born and raised in Charleston and kept a seaside cottage on Sullivan's Island. As is true in many Lowcountry homes still today, Poe's cottage had an insect problem—specifically an infestation of the cockroaches that we genteelly refer to as palmetto bugs. Poe's bug problem was a bit more extensive than a few roach motels could remedy. In fact, things got so bad that Poe's house was eventually completely overrun with roaches, until he awoke one night in terror to find his bed swarmed and his body pinned under the weight of a horde of bugs. Poe was overwhelmed physically and psychologically—the sensation of thousands of the insects' spindly legs crawling all over his body driving him to insanity.

The misinformed tour guide concluded his lecture by explaining that "The Gold-Bug" relayed this very tale of Poe's entomological-inspired descent into madness and was written in Poe's first-person narrator style because, like in all of Poe's classic tales, Poe is the narrator and he is relating firsthand, personal experiences.

As I watched the group walk to their car, I admit that I was a little conflicted. First, there was my knee-jerk reaction of head-shaking disappointment in the butchering of Poe history and the erroneous analysis of "The Gold-Bug." But then there was another part of me that found some measure of satisfaction in the fact that people were at least talking about Poe and his connection to Charleston, even if the specifics of their conversation were terribly, terribly inaccurate. And besides, it was probably unfair to judge too harshly the misguided Poe enthusiast who I observed that night. He certainly was not the first, nor will he be the last, to muddle Poe's facts with Poe's fiction.

The divide between Poe's real life and the experiences of his fictitious characters has long been blurred. The manic, unreliable, insistent and often psychotic narrators of many of his most macabre stories have been inextricably tied to and confused with the real Poe for as long as his work has been in print. And as Poe's life and mental health began to unravel in the last years of his life, he did in fact begin to display some of the unhinged traits and vulnerabilities of the psyche found in many of his story's narrators. The death of Virginia from tuberculosis on January 30, 1847, sent Poe's life into an alcohol-soaked tailspin, racked by depression and paranoia. An acquaintance recalled of Poe in the wake of Virginia's death, "He did not seem to care after she was gone, whether he lived an hour, a day, a week or a year; she was his all."

On November 4, 1848, Poe boarded a train in Providence, Rhode Island, bound for Boston, and upon his arrival in the city of his birth, he choked down what should have been a lethal dose of laudanum, but as he later described, "The laudanum was rejected from the stomach, I became calm, & to a casual observer, sane—so that I was suffered to go back to Providence."

The following summer in Philadelphia, while stumping for subscriptions for his ultimately unrealized *Stylus* magazine, Poe was arrested for public drunkenness. Released a few hours after the magistrate recognized his defendant and declared, "Why, this is Poe the poet," a still intoxicated and delusional Poe burst wildly into the office of editor John Sartain, screaming about a plot to kill him that he had overheard on a train.

A manic Poe said to Sartain, "If this moustache of mine were removed I should not be so readily recognized. Will you lend me a razor, that I may shave it off?"

Arguably the most famous portrait of Poe, the haunting 1848 *Ultima Thule Daguerreotype* was taken just four days after he attempted to take his own life with an overdose of laudanum. *Courtesy of the Edgar Allan Poe Museum, Richmond, Virginia.*

Virginia's death also meant the return of the torment of Poe's oldest of demons—his longing for female fostering and companionship. He spent his last years frantically chasing romance, and, as my wife characterizes my own bachelor lifestyle before meeting her, Poe became a "serial dater." He courted several ladies and proposed marriage to at least two different women in the last years of his life. An engagement to poet Sarah Helen

Whitman derailed when her requirement of sobriety proved a bridge too far for Poe. But in the autumn of 1849, while visiting Richmond, Poe ran into his old flame, the recently widowed Elmira Royster. Sparks flew once again between the pair, and Poe almost immediately proposed marriage. By the end of September, it was rumored in Richmond that Poe and Elmira were engaged, or at least had reached a cautious understanding, and Poe seemed improbably happy and hopeful for the first time in more than two years.

And what happened next? Nobody is quite sure. The Edgar Allan Poe story takes its most mysterious, debated and still unexplained turn.

On September 27, after bidding a melancholy farewell to Elmira, Poe, who Elmira described that day as "very sad, and complained of being quite sick," took a steamer from Richmond in the early morning hours to make passage north for business—first to Philadelphia to take a short, lucrative job that paid $100 for editing the poetry of a wealthy piano manufacturer's wife and then on to New York. But Poe never made it to Philadelphia, and on October 3, Dr. Joseph Snodgrass, a Baltimore literary friend of Poe, received an urgent note: "There is a gentleman, rather worse for the wear, at Ryan's 4th ward polls, who goes under the cognomen Edgar A. Poe, and who appears in great distress, & says he is acquainted with you, and I assure you, he is in need of immediate assistance."

Snodgrass found Poe semiconscious at a nearby bar, wearing someone else's soiled clothes and "utterly stupefied with liquor." He was taken to Washington College Hospital, where he became restless and spoke incoherently until the morning of October 5, when he suddenly told his doctor, "The best thing his friends could do would be to blow his brains out with a pistol." For the next two days, Poe alternated between sleep and violent delirium until the evening of October 6, when he mysteriously began calling out for several hours for someone named Reynolds. Poe rested for a short time before muttering, "Lord help my poor soul" and dying moments later in the early morning hours of October 7, 1849.

With little fanfare and fewer than a dozen people in attendance, Poe was buried the following day in an unmarked grave at Westminster Hall next to his grandfather, grandmother and brother. Speculation as to the cause of his mysterious death began almost immediately, and the subject has been famously debated for more than a century and a half. Baltimore newspapers reported the cause of death as "congestion of the brain" and "cerebral inflammation," but both terms were often used as euphemisms for alcoholism.

The French poet Charles Baudelaire, who famously spent seventeen years translating Poe's works, remarked laconically on his death, "This death was almost a suicide, a suicide prepared for a long time." If you type "Poe's death" into a search engine, you will find there is no shortage of theories from the ridiculous to the thought provoking to explain Poe's death, including exposure, lead poisoning, brain tumor, rabies, syphilis and even a Mafia-style hit by Elmira Royster's brothers, who were suspicious of Poe's intentions with their sister. The fact that Poe was found "utterly stupefied with liquor" outside the Fourth Ward Polls on Election Day in Baltimore produced perhaps the most popular and enduring of theories, that Poe was the victim of "cooping," an aggressive form of voter fraud popular among Baltimore's political gangs where a victim was plied with drink and forced to vote multiple times at different polling stations.

Whatever the cause, news of Poe's death traveled fast, and on October 9, one of the most infamous obituaries ever written appeared in the *New York Tribune* signed under the name Ludwig: "Edgar Allan Poe is dead....This announcement will startle many, but few will be grieved by it. The poet was known, personally or by reputation, in all this country; he had readers in England, and in several of the states of Continental Europe; but he had few or no friends."

Ludwig was really Rufus Wilmot Griswold, a failed Baptist minister turned editor. In 1842, Griswold had published a hugely successful anthology titled *The Poets and Poetry of America*, which featured poems from more than eighty American writers. A review written by Poe shortly after *The Poets and Poetry of America* was published was the genesis of the rift between Poe and Griswold and inspired Griswold to write his vicious obituary seven years later. Poe had contributed three poems to Griswold's anthology but was critical in his review, citing the collection's lack of southern writers and pointing to Griswold's "prepossession, evidently perceived by himself, for the writers of New England." The criticisms of Griswold's work were fairly mild for the "Tomahawk Man," but the sensitive Griswold remarked that Poe handled him "very sharply," and he never forgot the slight.

When Poe died, Griswold saw his chance to exact his revenge, and, through some less-than-ethical arrangements made with a cash-strapped Maria Clemm, he secured the rights to serve as Poe's literary executor. Griswold quickly followed his nasty obituary of Poe with the even more unflattering *Memoir of the Author*, a posthumous biographical sketch and collection of Poe's works that depicted Poe in the darkest of lights, as mad, chronically drunk and even addicted to drugs. *Memoir of the Author* was a clear act of character assassination, as Griswold manipulated and, when necessary, invented details of Poe's life to fit his slanderous narrative. Poe's not returning for a second term at the University of Virginia was recounted by Griswold as Poe being expelled for wild and reckless behavior, and Poe's discharge from the army was represented as desertion. Griswold was particularly preoccupied with Poe's finances and lost no opportunity to point out and dwell upon Poe's poverty. And in perhaps the

Rufus Wilmot Griswold.

most disturbing and outlandish passage of the memoir, Griswold implied that Poe had tried to seduce John Allan's second wife, Louisa.

Unfortunately for Poe, Griswold's grim October 9 obituary in the *New York Tribune* was picked up and printed in newspapers all over the country. Even more unfortunate for Poe, Griswold's scandalous *Memoir of the Author* was widely read and was the only readily available biography of Poe for the first twenty-five years after his death. As proof of the power of first impressions, much of the way that we remember and envision Poe still today is anchored in those very aspersions penned by Griswold. His depiction has transcended generations and imprinted a lasting, though not necessarily accurate, legacy of Poe.

In 1860, Neilson Poe ordered a marble headstone to be placed at his famous cousin's still unmarked grave, but in a remarkable story that supports the notion that fact is stranger than fiction, the stone was destroyed before it could be installed when a train ran off its tracks and barreled into the yard where the new headstone was being stored. Five years later, a movement under the leadership of Sara Sigourney Rice began in Baltimore to raise money for a new monument to mark Poe's grave and honor the city's neglected poet. Poe's remains were exhumed and reinterred in a more visible and accessible section of the graveyard, and the new monument was dedicated on November 17, 1875. Made of marble, the monument stands about six and a half feet tall and features a bas-relief of Poe on its face. Virginia was exhumed from her grave in New York, and she and Maria Clemm, who died in 1871, were laid to rest next to Poe. The unorthodox little family was finally back together.

The dedication of Poe's monument at his grave in Baltimore in 1875 marked the beginning of a century-and-a-half explosion of the dedications of monuments, plaques, tributes and historic sites honoring Poe in various cities seeking to claim Poe as their own. Richmond dedicated the Poe shrine in 1922, which eventually became the Poe Museum. Poe's rented home in Philadelphia was designated as the Edgar Allan Poe National Historic Site in 1962. The cottage Poe shared with Virginia and Maria in New York is a museum operated by the Bronx County Historical Society. And Baltimore honors Poe with no less than a professional football team—the Baltimore Ravens.

And then there is Charleston.

The Charleston shrine to Poe to attract "half a million visitors each year" that Caroline Leland called for in her 1969 letter has not yet materialized. Vestiges of Poe in the Lowcountry are few and far between. But if you are intent on finding Poe, I will offer you a little guide. The best place to start looking for Poe is on his former island home—Sullivan's Island.

If you visit Sullivan's Island via Mount Pleasant, Poe makes an appearance before you have even crossed the Ben Sawyer Bridge onto the island. A sign at the foot of the bridge directs you down a gentle, worn asphalt slope to Gold Bug Island. The small island set in a tidal marsh alongside the Intracoastal Waterway was purchased in 1957 by a group of water and boating enthusiasts calling themselves the East Cooper Outboard Club. To honor their island's namesake, the group adopted a yellow and black bug with large pincers as their official symbol and set about building a boat ramp and clubhouse on the island. The island suffered major damage during Hurricane Hugo in 1989, and eight years later, it was placed in a conservation easement with the Lowcountry Open Land Trust to protect the island and prevent future development. Today, the East Cooper Outboard Motor Club rents the clubhouse as an event facility, and Gold Bug Island has become particularly popular for hosting oyster roasts.

Once on Sullivan's Island, you quickly reach the intersection of Middle Street, where pedestrian traffic suddenly swells, jaywalking becomes the norm and golf carts nearly outnumber cars. Just around the corner from this busy intersection sits what is, for most Charleston locals, the most clear and direct connection to Edgar Allan Poe—Poe's Tavern. That the local site most associated with Poe is a bar is rich with irony. And I am certain that if Poe's Tavern had been open in 1828, Edgar A. Perry would have been a regular. Poe's drinking is the stuff of legend, but in all fairness to Poe, he did try to get off the sauce, joining the local chapter of Richmond's Sons of

Temperance a little over a month before his mysterious death—apparently with some substandard results.

Opened in 2003, Poe's Tavern is a Poe lover's dream. Poe images are everywhere, and once you step inside, his eyes never seem to leave you. Portraits, movie posters, advertisements and newspaper clippings hang from walls that are papered with his prose and poetry. Even the menu pays tribute to Poe, offering burgers with names inspired by his most popular tales, like "The Pit and the Pendulum," "Tell-Tale Heart" and, of course, "The Gold-Bug." Poe even follows you to the restroom, where you would be forgiven if you mistakenly believed that James Earl Jones or the late Vincent Price occupied the stall next to you, as the tavern pipes a constant stream of readings of Poe's works over the bathroom speakers. The focal point of the restaurant is a mural above the fireplace near the bar, in which Poe's countenance appears unusually relaxed, even peaceful. But in the "rare event indeed when a fire is considered necessary," the glow of a crackling fire seems to reveal the more familiar brooding and melancholic Poe.

Traveling west on Middle Street to the western tip of the island, you will find the austere walls of Fort Moultrie and its National Park Service visitors' center. You might expect the fort to celebrate its most famous former resident and stand as one of Poe's most enduring monuments, but you would be wrong. There are no signs or plaques inside the fort declaring "Poe slept here" and no Poe T-shirts or stuffed ravens can be found for sale in the gift shop. I expected to at least find a token wax figure of a uniformed Poe scribbling at a desk in the visitors' center, but besides a Poe brochure with a brief summary of his time stationed at the fort and the brick near the sally port etched with the initials EAP that turned out to be a fraud, there are no traces of Poe to be found at Fort Moultrie. But perhaps there is hope for more Poe in Fort Moultrie's future. Shortly before I handed my manuscript to my editor, a bill was approved by Congress and signed by the president to change the designation of Fort Moultrie from merely part of the Fort Sumter National Monument to the higher-profile title of the Fort Sumter and Fort Moultrie National Park. Perhaps the nomination as a national park and the expected lift in profile and visibility will inspire and usher in a newfound spirit of recognition and commemoration of Poe.

Tracing a string of early twentieth-century military batteries that flank the eastern side of Fort Moultrie, what is probably the most appropriate of local tributes to Poe stands on I'On Avenue—the Edgar Allan Poe Library. A branch of the Charleston County Library, the Edgar Allan Poe library is uniquely housed in a renovated Spanish-American War–era four-gun

The author enjoying dinner under Poe's watchful gaze at Poe's Tavern. This portrait of Poe is just one of the dozens of Poe pictures, movie posters and advertisements that can be found covering the walls of the tavern. *Photo by Tina Downey.*

battery. At the library's opening ceremony on March 11, 1977, County Council chairman Lonnie Hamilton III noted the unusual use of the former military installation for a library, quoting Isaiah 2:4, "They shall beat their swords into ploughshares." The tight confines and low ceiling of the gun battery give a charming, perhaps slightly claustrophobic, vibe to the library, and Poe seems right at home with Poe-themed drawings, figurines, ravens and even a bust of Pallas filling the nooks and ledges among the stacks.

The last stop for those looking for Poe on Sullivan's Island requires a deeper exploration of the island. The streets on Sullivan's Island form a quasi-grid, with streets that run from north to south named after stations (Station 20, Station 21, etc.) intersected by quiet, shaded streets, including a few named to honor Poe, like Raven, Gold Bug and Poe Avenues. Near the intersection of Station 27 and Gold Bug Avenue, the world's oldest monument to Poe can be found—a monstrous ancient oak tree known by locals as the Gold Bug tree. Upon a first glance, it is easy to mistakenly think that you are viewing a grouping of tightly spaced trees rather than just one lone oak, but it really, truly is just one enormous tree, and it completely swallows the yard in which it sits.

The day that I visited to take pictures for this book, it had just begun to drizzle rain, and I found two young girls taking shelter in the tree's massive gnarled branches. "Is this your tree?" I asked.

"No," they replied, "it is Uncle Billy's." A few minutes later, as I was pacing the side of the street, trying to determine the best angle from which to fit as much of the huge tree into my camera frame, a truck pulled up and the girls began to chant, "Uncle Billy! Uncle Billy!"

I introduced myself to Uncle Billy and apologized for standing awkwardly in front of his house. Uncle Billy could not have been friendlier, and in his soft, coastal Carolina drawl, he explained that people have been coming to visit the tree for as long as he could remember. He bought the house in 1970 but had lived on Gold Bug Avenue his whole life. Uncle Billy spoke endearingly of the tree and obviously took its preservation seriously. "Lots of people have offered to cut-back the limbs, but I won't let them," he told me. I explained that I was writing a book on Poe and asked if it was okay to add a picture of his tree, since "The Gold-Bug" is one of the most important links between the Lowcountry and Poe. "Sure," he answered. And then with a smile stretching across his face, he said, "But I will tell you—I have been all over and around that tree and I haven't found any treasure."

Since Poe did not include a veritable X to mark the spot of the treasure in "The Gold-Bug," it is not surprising that Sullivan's Island is not the only locality to claim Poe's famous tree. On neighboring Isle of Palms, another giant oak that grows near the fairway of the long par five fourteenth hole of the Wild Dunes Links Course has also been declared to be the Gold Bug tree. This tree even comes with its own ghost—the apparition of Poe or perhaps a pirate—reported to be seen lingering near the tree. Not to be outdone, Mount Pleasant has laid claim to the Gold Bug tree as well, with some amateur treasure hunters who have used the clues of Poe's cryptogram, speculating that the treasure should be found beneath a large oak tree near the intersection of Highway 17 and Mathis Ferry Road.

But, of course, there is one problem with all these possible Gold Bug trees—the tree in Poe's story was actually a tulip tree, not an oak. But far be it from this author to ruin the fun of a good, old-fashioned treasure hunt.

Across the harbor in downtown Charleston, finding Poe is a little more challenging. On Meeting Street, not far from the market, there is an unexpected and all too infrequently visited tribute to Poe inside one of Charleston's finest hotels—the Belmond Charleston Place. Passing through the hotel's Italian marble lobby and ascending the sweeping Georgian staircase to the second floor, you will reach a long hallway that is a hall of fame of locals, known as Portraits of Charleston. Opposing walls are

The famed Gold Bug tree on Sullivan's Island. *Photo by Jennifer Taylor.*

filled with framed pictures honoring famous South Carolinians from Darius Rucker, front man of Hootie and the Blowfish, to former Charleston mayor Joseph P. Riley. A portrait of Edgar Allan Poe proudly hangs there as well. When I visited Portraits of Charleston, I found Poe flanked by civil rights activist Septima Poinsette Clark and South Carolina's thirty-sixth governor, Thomas Pickney. Poe's eyes somberly gaze across the hallway and appear locked in a never-ending staring contest with a seemingly unsuspecting, but still distinguished looking, Lord Proprietor Anthony Ashley Cooper.

A few blocks north on Meeting Street, another hotel, the King Charles Inn, has a long tradition of claiming Poe as one of its guests back when it was known as the Pavilion Hotel in the nineteenth century. The assertion does not necessarily have any documented proof, but I suppose it is entirely possible that while on furlough in the city, Poe may have spent the night there.

An Edgar Allan Poe walking tour that starts at the King Charles Inn celebrates the hotel's and several other nearby sites' potential connection to Poe, and I joined a mother and daughter visiting from Alabama for a tour on a cool autumn evening just a couple of days after Halloween. Our small tour group slipped through quiet neighborhoods off the main streets and made stops at the obvious Poe sites like the Unitarian Church, where our tour guide regaled us with the legend of Annabel Lee. We also visited several other sites that may have influenced Poe that I had not considered before, like the Old City Jail. It does not require too big of a leap of faith to believe Poe may have been influenced by its austere, fortressed walls when writing "The Pit and the Pendulum." At the northeast corner of Broad and Meeting Streets, we craned our necks and peered up at the steeple of St. Michael's Church, where the tolling bells have a long local tradition of being the inspiration for Poe's poem "The Bells."

Another, more nefarious, legend linking Poe to St. Michael's tells of creepy, grim reaper–like shadows cast as the setting sun beams through St. Michael's iconic spire. Perhaps Poe seized upon this legend in "The City in the Sea," with the lines, "While from a proud tower in the town, Death looks gigantically down." At First Scots Presbyterian Church on Meeting Street, the legend of an unfortunate young man named George Woodrop may have served as the inspiration for some of Poe's most terrifying stories, like "The Premature Burial" and "The Cask of Amontillado," which featured Poe's infamous preoccupation with being buried alive. At Woodrop's funeral in 1770, there seemed to have been some debate as to whether the young man was actually dead. When Woodrop's coffin was accidentally breached nine years later while digging an adjacent grave, the church's sexton, John

Mills, was horrified to find Woodrop's body unnaturally positioned in its coffin. Louisa Susannah Wells, whose father had been at Woodrop's funeral, recorded Mill's chilling discovery, "He [Mills] opened the grave, uncovered the lid of the coffin, and found the deceased lying on its side, with the cheekbone in the palm of the hand!"

Our guide faced many of the same obstacles in conducting our tour that I have had in writing this book, namely the shortage of proven, substantiated or otherwise documented evidence of Poe's life and experiences during his time in Charleston. But the route of our tour did create a melancholic, dark, Poe-like mood as we left the main streets and wound through old neighborhoods, offering a unique perspective of a Charleston not much changed from when Poe walked the same streets nearly two centuries ago. As we walked, I was reminded of one of the first results I found when I typed "Edgar Allan Poe Charleston" into a search engine at the start of my research, and it seems a fitting way to conclude. It is from the first page of *The Lords of Discipline* by Pat Conroy, who also happens to be honored on the Belmond Charleston Place's Portraits of Charleston. The passage comes from the story's narrator, Will McLean, and the words have resonated with me from my first reading. They seemed particularly poignant that evening of my tour as I walked in Poe's footsteps in Charleston:

> *I am not a son of Charleston. Nor could I be if I wanted to. I am always a visitor, and my allegiance lies with other visitors, sons and daughters of accident and circumstance. Edgar Allan Poe was a son by visitation. It was no surprise to me when I was a freshman at the Institute to discover that Poe was once stationed at Fort Moultrie and that he wrote "The Gold-Bug" about one of the sea islands near Charleston. I like to think of him walking the streets of Charleston as I walked them, and it pleases me to think that the city watched him, felt the shimmer of his madness and genius in his slouching promenades along Meeting Street. I like to think of the city shaping this agitated, misplaced soldier, keening his passion for shade, trimming the soft edges of his nightmare, harshening the poisons and his metaphors, deepening his intimacy with the sunless wastes that issued forth from his kingdom of nightmare in blazing islands still inchoate and unformed, of the English language. Whenever I go back to Charleston, I think of Poe.*

Bibliography

Abugel, Jeffrey. *Edgar Allan Poe's Petersburg: The Untold Story of the Raven in the Cockade City*. Charleston, SC: The History Press, 2013.

Allen, Hervey. *Israfel: The Life and Times of Edgar Allan Poe*. 1926. Reprint. New York: Farrar and Rinehart, 1934.

Brown, Michael. "Pleasing Terrors." November 18, 2016. In *The Mourner's Curse*. Edited by Mike Shear. MP3 audio. 37:26. https://pleasingterrors. libsyn.com.

Collins, Paul. *Edgar Allan Poe: The Fever Called Living*. Boston, MA: Houghton Mifflin Harcourt, 2014.

Conroy, Pat. *The Lords of Discipline*. Boston, MA: Houghton Mifflin Harcourt, 1980.

Curtis, Mary Julia. "The Early Charleston Stage: 1703–1798." PhD diss., Indiana University, 1968.

Dormon, James H. *Theater in the Ante-Bellum South, 1815–1861*. Chapel Hill: University of North Carolina Press, 1967.

Harris, Benjamin S.H. "Edgar Allan Poe's Stay on Sullivan's Island." *South Carolina Magazine*, Summer 1975.

Heyward, DuBose, and Hervey Allen. *Carolina Chansons: Legends of the Low Country*. New York: Macmillan, 1922.

Hoole, William Stanley. *The Ante-Bellum Charleston Theatre*. Tuscaloosa: University of Alabama Press, 1946.

———. "Poe in Charleston, S.C." *American Literature* 6, no. 1 (March 1934–January 1935): 78–80.

———. "Two Famous Theatres of the Old South." *South Atlantic Quarterly* 36 (July 1937): 273–75.

Hutchisson, James M. *Poe.* Jackson: University Press of Mississippi, 2005.

Jones, Mark R., ed. *Kingdom by the Sea: Edgar Allan Poe's Charleston Tales.* Charleston, SC: East Atlantic Publishing, 2013.

Kennedy, J. Gerald, ed. *A Historical Guide to Edgar Allan Poe.* New York: Oxford University Press, 2001.

Kibler, James Everett, Jr., and David Moltke-Hansen. *William Gilmore Simms's Selected Reviews on Literature and Civilization.* Columbia: University of South Carolina Press, 2014.

Law, Robert Adger. "A Source for Annabel Lee." *Journal of English and Germanic Philology* 21, no. 2 (April 1922): 341–46.

Meyers, Jeffrey. *Edgar Allan Poe: His Life and Legacy.* New York: Scribner, 1992.

Miles, Suzannah Smith. "Lost Pirate Treasure Still Unfound?" *Moultrie News.* October 13, 2015.

———. "Love, Loss, and Lore: Searching for Poe's 'Kingdom by the Sea' and the Real-Life Legrand." *Charleston Magazine,* July–August 2003.

Neely, Jack. "Tracking Poe's Past." *Charleston Magazine,* October–November 1993.

Ocker, J.W. *Poe-Land: The Hallowed Haunts of Edgar Allan Poe.* New York: Countryman Press, 2015.

Ostrom, John W., Burton R. Pollin, and Jeffrey A. Savoye, eds. *The Collected Letters of Edgar Allan Poe in 2 Volumes.* 3rd ed. New York: Gordian Press, 2008.

Peeples, Scott. *The Afterlife of Edgar Allan Poe.* Rochester, NY: Camden House, 2004.

———. *Edgar Allan Poe Revisited.* New York, Twayne, 1998.

Peeples, Scott, and Michelle Van Parys. "Unburied Treasure: Edgar Allan Poe and the South Carolina Lowcountry." *Southern Cultures* 22, no. 2 (Summer 2016).

Poe, Edgar Allan. *Edgar Allan Poe: Complete Tales and Poems.* New York: Fall River Press, 2012.

———. *The Fall of the House of Usher and Other Writings.* New York: Penguin, 1986.

———. *The Gold-Bug.* Charleston, SC: Tradd Street Press, 1969.

Quinn, Arthur Hobson. *Edgar Allan Poe: A Critical Biography.* 1941. Reprint. Baltimore, MD: Johns Hopkins University Press, 1998.

Ravenel, Beatrice Witte. *The Arrow of Lightning*. New York: Harold Vinal, 1926.

Russell, J. Thomas. *Edgar Allan Poe: The Army Years*. West Point, NY: U.S. Military Academy, 1972.

Seibels, Genie. "Poe on Sullivan's Island." *Literary Traveler*, October 4, 2002.

Silverman, Kenneth. *Edgar A. Poe: Mournful and Never-ending Remembrance*. New York: Harper Collins, 1991.

Smith, Geddeth. *The Brief Career of Eliza Poe*. Cranbury, NJ: Associated University Press, 1988.

Smyth, Ellison A., Jr. "Poe's Gold Bug from the Standpoint of an Entomologist." *Sewanee Review* 17, no. 1 (January 1910): 67–72.

Sodders, Richard P. "The Theatre Management of Alexandre Placide in Charleston, 1794–1812." 2 vols. PhD diss., Louisiana State University, 1983.

Stange, Eric, dir. *Edgar A. Poe: Buried Alive*. Arlington, MA: Spy Pond Productions, 2017.

Stevenson, Robert Louis. *Treasure Island*. New York: Bantam Books, 1992.

Thomas, Dwight, and David K. Jackson, eds. *The Poe Log: A Documentary Life of Edgar Allan Poe*. Boston, MA: G.K. Hall, 1987.

Trent, William P. *William Gilmore Simms*. New York: Haskell House, 1968.

Willis, Eola. *The Charleston Stage in the 18th Century*. Columbia, SC: State Company, 1924.

Index

O

Osceola 51
Osgood, Frances 94

P

Penn Magazine 62
Placide, Alexandre 18, 20, 21, 22,
    26, 28, 29, 32, 34, 98
Poe, David 28, 29, 30, 31, 32, 40,
    120
Poe, Eliza Arnold 23, 25, 26, 27,
    28, 29, 30, 31, 32, 33, 34, 35,
    40
Poe Museum (Richmond, Virginia)
    115, 116, 128
Poe, Rosalie 32, 33, 34, 40
Poe Sr., General David 49
Poe's Tavern 85, 121, 128, 129
Poetry Society of South Carolina
    116, 117, 118
Poe, Virginia Clemm 63, 64, 65,
    68, 94, 123, 124, 127, 128
Poe, William Henry 30, 32, 34, 40,
    41, 44, 47, 57, 62

R

Ravenel, Beatrice Witte 120
Ravenel, Dr. Edmund 75, 76, 77,
    78, 87, 88
Raven Society 34
Richmond Theatre 30, 33, 34, 58
Royster, Elmira 43, 44, 56, 88, 125

S

Shockoe Hill Cemetery 58
Simms, William Gilmore 104, 105,
    106, 107, 108, 109, 110, 111,
    113, 114
Smith, Alice Ravenel Huger 117
Sollee, John 15, 16, 17, 18, 19, 20,
    21, 22, 23, 25, 26, 33, 98
Southern Literary Messenger, the 63,
    65, 66, 67, 68, 94, 108, 111,
    114
Southern Patriot 108
Southern Review 57, 77
Stanard, Jane 42, 43, 58, 94
Stevenson, Robert Louis 75
Stylus magazine 62, 123
Sullivan's Island 37, 39, 49, 57, 70,
    71, 74, 75, 77, 80, 85, 86, 87,
    88, 106, 116, 119, 121, 122,
    128, 131

T

Timrod, Henry 110, 111, 112, 113
Tubbs, Charles 15, 20, 21, 22, 23, 24
Tubbs, Elizabeth Arnold 23, 25, 28

U

Unitarian Church 82, 84, 85, 86,
    87, 88, 89, 90, 92, 93, 133
United States Military Academy at
    West Point 58, 59, 63, 66,
    67, 115
University of Virginia 34, 44, 46,
    67, 127

About the Author

Christopher Byrd Downey (Captain Byrd) received his degree in history from Virginia Tech in 1995 and shortly after graduating began a career in the maritime industry. He has previously authored two books on the history of piracy in South Carolina, *Stede Bonnet: Charleston's Gentleman Pirate* and *Charleston and the Golden Age of Piracy*. A native of Virginia, he now lives in Charleston with his wife, Tina, and son, Sailor. Visit him at www.captainbyrds.com.